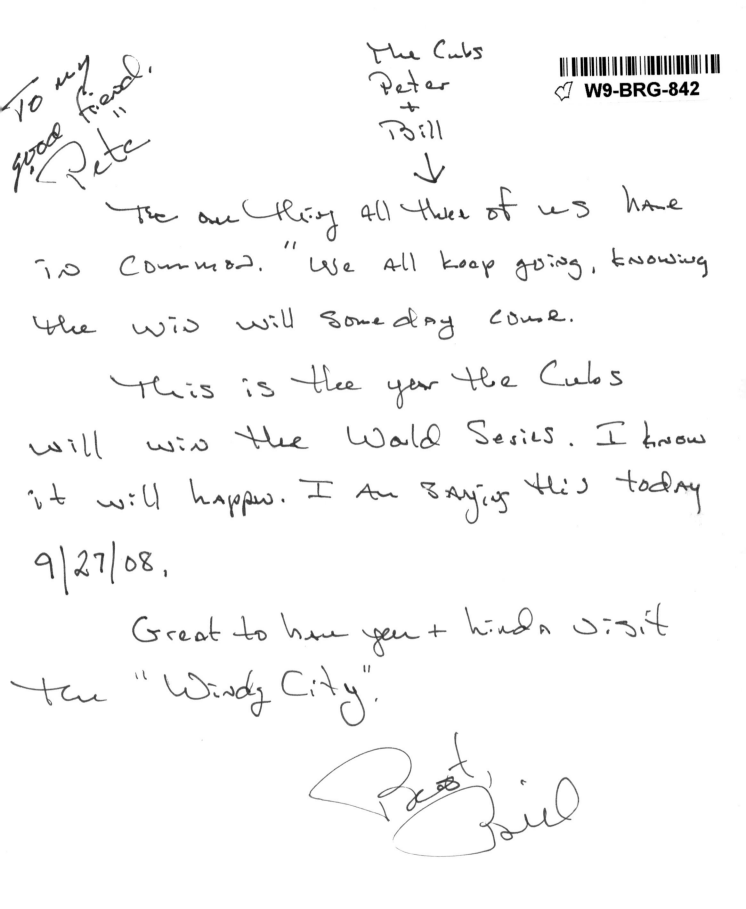

To my good friend "Pete"

The Cubs
Peter
+
Bill
↓

The one thing all three of us have in common. "We all keep going, knowing the win will someday come.

This is the year the Cubs will win the World Series. I know it will happen. I am saying this today 9/27/08.

Great to have you + Linda visit the "Windy City".

Best,
Bill

⎔ W9-BRG-842

With etymological roots dating to the 1800s, "hoodoo" refers to someone or something believed to bring bad luck. As in:

JINX

HEX

or

CURSE

Hoodoo \Hoo"doo\ (h[=oo]"d[=oo]), n. [Perh. a var. of voodoo.]
1. One who causes bad luck. [Colloq.]
[1913 Webster]

2. Same as voodoo.

3. Bad luck.

Hoodoo \Hoo"doo\, v. t.
To be a hoodoo to; to bring bad luck to by occult influence;
to bewitch. [Colloq., U. S.]
[Webster 1913 Suppl.]

HOODOO

UNRAVELING THE 100-YEAR-OLD MYSTERY OF THE CHICAGO CUBS

By Grant DePorter, Elliott Harris, and Mark Vancil

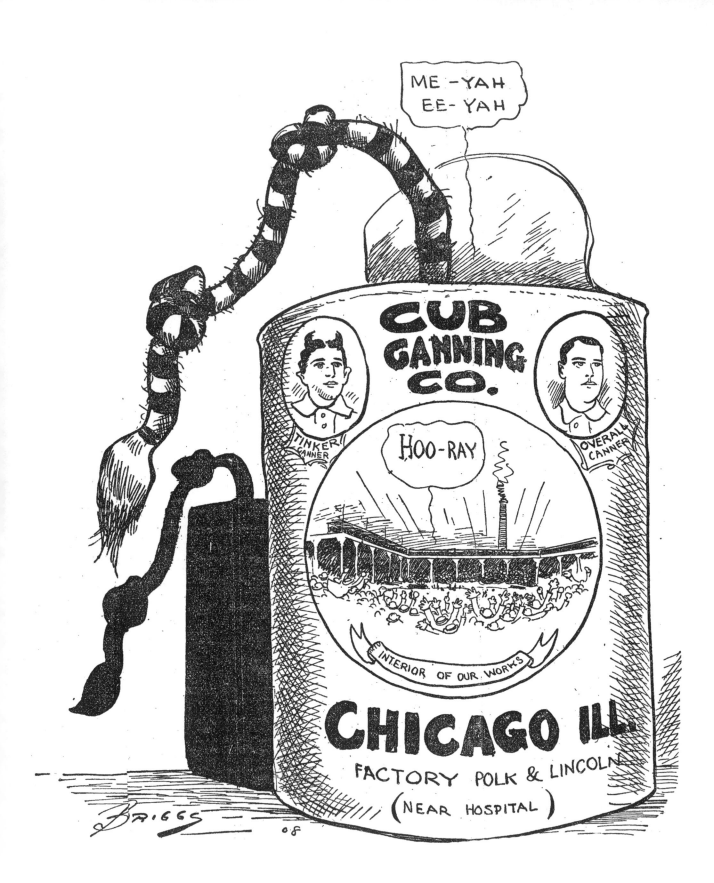

TABLE OF CONTENTS

RARE AIR BOOKS
A Division of Rare Air Media

Compilation copyright © 2008 by Rare Air, Ltd.

Library of Congress Cataloging–in–Publication Data is available upon request
ISBN: 978-0-9820512-0-7

First Rare Air Books Hardcover Edition September 2008
10 9 8 7 6 5 4 3 2
Rare Air is a registered trademark of Rare Air, Ltd.
www.rareairmedia.com

Designed by Vieceli Design
Created and Produced by Rare Air Books

Printed and bound in the United States of America

For information regarding special discounts for bulk purchases,
please contact us on the World Wide Web

CUBSHOODOO.COM

ACKNOWLEDGEMENTS

There are certain people I would like to acknowledge: my wife Joanna, who works alongside me at Harry Caray's and was instrumental in writing this book. Dutchie Caray, for her unbelievable support these last ten years. Cubs Hall of Famer Ryne Sandberg, Marty Cohn, and St. Louis Cardinals owner Nick Kladis (even though he decided to buy the wrong team). Harry Caray's director of marketing Beth Heller, Carol Sterling, Rick Simon, and Irwin Jann. Sun-Times columnist Mike Sneed, who covered the foul-ball events from beginning to end better than anyone else. Sun-Times cartoonist Jack Higgins who is the best in his business and graciously lent his works to this book. Cubs Hall of Famer "Mr. Cub" Ernie Banks, Chairman of the West Side Rooters Social Club. John McDonough, Chicago Blackhawks President and former Cubs President, for being a close friend and mentor. Jay Blunk, Blackhawks Sr. Vice President and former Cubs Sr. Vice President of Marketing, for his friendship and never-ending support. My twelve-year-old twin daughters Margo and Hannah. Both are huge Cubs fans, and both threw strikes with their ceremonial first pitches at a Cubs vs. Cardinals game when they were six years old. And a special thanks to Cubs Chairman Crane Kenney; General Manager Jim Hendry; Assistant General Manager Randy Bush; Executive Vice President of Business Operations Mark McGuire; Senior Vice President of Community Affairs Mike Lufrano; Director of Promotion and Sales Matt Wszolek; Manager of Special Events, Player Relations, and Entertainment Joe Rios; and Senior Account Executive Andrea Burke, for their support over the years.

Finally, this book would not have been possible without the help of Cubs fan and friend Bill Loughman. Bill turned over to me his priceless newspaper collection dating back to 1876, and all he wanted in return was free corned beef sandwiches for life.

◎ ◎ ◎ GRANT DEPORTER ◎ ◎ ◎

Thanking the following people for their assistance with this book doesn't even begin to tell the story. To Sue, Rachel, and Mark Harris—no man could have a more encouraging wife, daughter, and son. Your patience and understanding during this undertaking made the project that much more enjoyable. To Marvin and Rosemary Harris, who taught their son about the wonder of words. To Robert Harris, an all-star catcher and a Hall of Fame brother who always provided a healthy dose of reality. To Robert Kurson, a great author and an even better friend. Robert's ability to comprehend and explain how writing, life, and baseball intersect is unsurpassed. Conversing with him provided broad beacons of illumination when this author sometimes was struggling in the dark. To those who traveled back to 1908 and provided information and insights: Brian Bernardoni, Jonathan Eig, Ed Hartig, Rick Kaempfer, Kathleen Murphy, and Tim Wiles. To all who dream and work to make that dream come true.

◎ ◎ ◎ ELLIOTT HARRIS ◎ ◎ ◎

From the first time I met Grant DePorter on through every minute of the countless hours we spent putting together this book, the experience was as enjoyable as it was illuminating. The passion that Grant and Joanna have for the Cubs is matched only by the care they give to people who share that passion. The warmth of their approach to people and business is why Harry Caray's Italian Steakhouse is called Chicago Cubs' home plate. And it's why Harry's name will forever be in good hands.

Elliott Harris, an old friend, helped bring the project to life. He agreed to turn his vacation into what no doubt felt like a never-ending succession of long nights researching, writing, and note-taking.

And in a schedule squeezed beyond reason, John Vieceli's work ethic and talent became the glue that held this book together. As always, even the most unreasonable request was met with nothing more than, "Is that it?" Once more, John's friendship, humor, and intelligence made the process a joy.

At home, as the days turned into nights and the nights turned back into days, Laura and our children—Alexandra, Samantha, Isabella, and my boy, Jonah—never failed to brighten every moment and pick up whatever pieces fell in my absence. I remain humbled by their warmth, beauty, and wonder.

◎ ◎ ◎ MARK VANCIL ◎ ◎ ◎

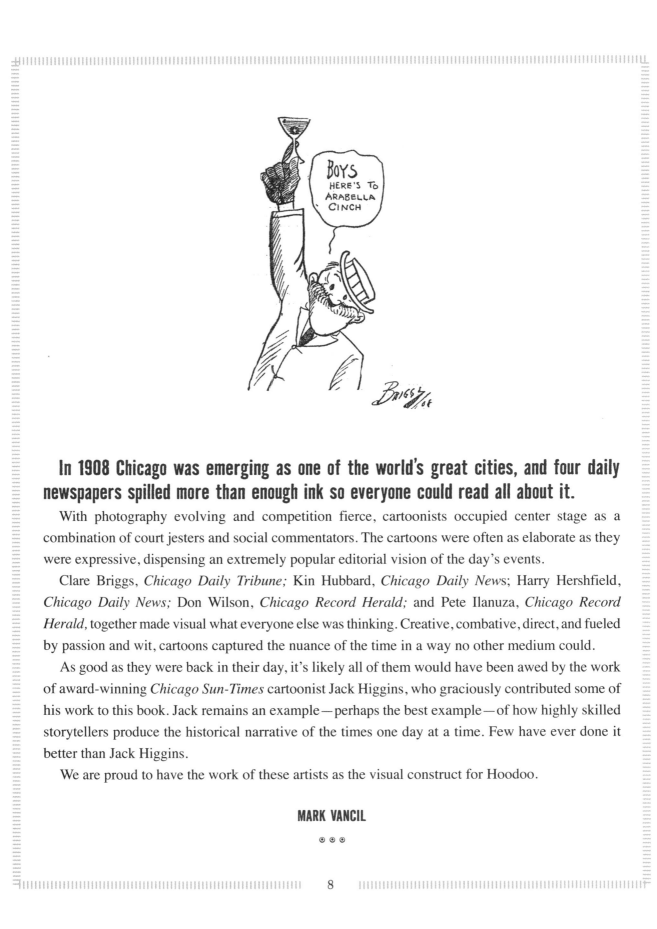

In 1908 Chicago was emerging as one of the world's great cities, and four daily newspapers spilled more than enough ink so everyone could read all about it.

With photography evolving and competition fierce, cartoonists occupied center stage as a combination of court jesters and social commentators. The cartoons were often as elaborate as they were expressive, dispensing an extremely popular editorial vision of the day's events.

Clare Briggs, *Chicago Daily Tribune;* Kin Hubbard, *Chicago Daily New*s; Harry Hershfield, *Chicago Daily News;* Don Wilson, *Chicago Record Herald;* and Pete Ilanuza, *Chicago Record Herald,* together made visual what everyone else was thinking. Creative, combative, direct, and fueled by passion and wit, cartoons captured the nuance of the time in a way no other medium could.

As good as they were back in their day, it's likely all of them would have been awed by the work of award-winning *Chicago Sun-Times* cartoonist Jack Higgins, who graciously contributed some of his work to this book. Jack remains an example—perhaps the best example—of how highly skilled storytellers produce the historical narrative of the times one day at a time. Few have ever done it better than Jack Higgins.

We are proud to have the work of these artists as the visual construct for Hoodoo.

MARK VANCIL

◉ ◉ ◉

THE BASEBALL CIRCUS.

GLOSSARY

Over time, words, the meaning of words and even their spelling evolve. In 1908, there were a number of words—including those below—that cartoonists and writers used to convey thoughts and feelings inconsistent with the way that word is used in 2008. For example, the word "gay" was used to convey happiness and had no other connotation. In other cases, words such as Pittsburg were simply spelled differently then and evolved into the modern spelling. There are other words in the cartoons and news accounts in this book that might appear as though they are being misused or misspelled. It is more likely the word was simply spelled differently one hundred years ago.

BENEDICT = a married male, a traitor to bachelorhood. The term was a reference to Revolutionary War traitor Benedict Arnold.

BUGS = fans (depicted in cartoon as insect-like creatures)

LAKESIDE BUGS = Chicago Cubs fans

CINCH = clinch

GAY = happy

HOODOO DETECTIVE = one who recognizes curses

OXYGEN CREAM = hydrogen peroxide

PEACH = a good person

PROGRAMME = program

SALOON = bar

SCIENTIFIC ROOTING = organized cheering

TALLYHO PARTY = parade to the park

TO-DAY = today

TO-MORROW = tomorrow

URSINE COLOSSI = another name for the Cubs

WORLD'S SERIES = World Series

AIR LINER = Airplane

PITTSBURG = Pittsburgh; the town was known as Pittsburg from 1890-1911

MR. JENSEN WON THE MARATHON SWIMMING RACE IN A WALK

CHAPTER 1

HOODOO

UNRAVELING THE MYSTERY OF THE CHICAGO CUBS

◉ ◉ ◉

This is the story of how a hoodoo that afflicted the Chicago Cubs for more than one hundred years was revealed and ultimately—we believe—exorcized by Cubs fans around the world through a series of discoveries, rituals, and hoodoo-cleansing events.

It is a story of goats, black cats, Red Sox and White Sox, superstitions, at least one incredible account of voodoo, countless hoodoos, artifacts, history foretold by Nostradamus, and coincidence, uncovered in an archeological dig through one-hundred-year-old yellowed newsprint.

Ultimately it's about one man's carelessness, and how loose lips and arrogance initiated a hoodoo of epic proportions, an act so utterly egregious that it trumped a remarkable World Series run, and for one hundred years thereafter forbade another.

As we have found (and you will see) everything that has happened to the Chicago Cubs—from their 1945 World Series failure to their 1969 collapse, to the infamous foul ball in the 2003 playoffs—reverts to a single source in 1908, Hoodoo Ground Zero for Cubs fans near and far.

The story starts where only it could: with

Harry Caray.

◉ ◉ ◉

INTRODUCTION BY GRANT DEPORTER

IN SEARCH OF HOODOO

On an otherwise nondescript December day in 2001, I walked through Harry Caray's Italian Steakhouse and Bar, as I had thousands of times before. I walked through the hallway leading from the restaurant into the bar, past hundreds of photos and artifacts of Harry and the Chicago Cubs. As president of Harry Caray's Restaurant Group, I knew Harry as a business partner and friend, an experience of a magnitude few could appreciate outside the Cubs universe. On this day, I was preparing for another Toast to Harry, talking out loud about plans and preparations.

73,000
BUDWEISERS
IN A LIFETIME

As I approached the bar, a cocktail waitress turned in my direction and looked directly into my eyes.

"A thought just popped into my head," she said. "You should take the Toast to Harry international and start by calling a place called the No Name Café in Puerto Vallarta, Mexico."

She was referring to the Toast to Harry Caray, an iconic event that we started following his death. The whole thing had grown organically, thanks to Cubs fans and sports-related venues around the country. The idea was to honor Harry in a way he would have appreciated, with a wink toward heaven and the hope that in some way we might invoke his spirit to remove whatever hoodoo or hex had been put on the Cubs. Like everyone else, we knew there was something at work beyond what we could see. And like everyone else, we had no idea what it was.

Besides, what better way to salute Harry than with a glass of beer?

What better way for Cubs fans to create good karma for the upcoming season than to salute him, and by doing so to hope he might be able to influence the baseball gods with whom he undoubtedly was swapping stories and drinking beer?

That's why the Toast to Harry Caray was created. To be sure, Harry was far more than a Hall of Fame broadcaster. When he died on February 18, 1998, there was a tremendous void. At the restaurant. At Wrigley Field. In the world.

Dutchie, Harry's widow, filled that void wonderfully on Opening Day at Wrigley, April 3, 1998, by leading the crowd in a rousing rendition of "Take Me Out to the Ball Game." Bagpipers played

"Amazing Grace," and thousands of balloons were released over the field in tribute to Harry.

The 1998 season featured moments that Harry would have loved: rookie Kerry Wood striking out twenty Houston Astros on May 6, and Sammy Sosa hitting a Major League Baseball-record twenty home runs in June. Sammy pointed skyward after each of his sixty-six homers that season in tribute to Harry. The Cubs won a one-game playoff against the San Francisco Giants to earn the National League wild-card entry in the postseason. A Harry ghost balloon loomed over the Wrigley bleachers in the postseason, one that ended for the Cubs with a loss, as all other postseasons had for the team since 1908. What a season for Harry to miss. What a season to miss Harry. A patch with Harry's caricature was sewn on to all Cubs uniforms.

To mark the one-year anniversary of his death, the restaurant invited fans to participate in the first Toast to Harry, on February 18, 1999. A year later, sports-related restaurants around the country participated in the Toast. The goal was for 73,000 fans to raise a drink in his memory. Why 73,000? Because Harry said he drank 73,000 Budweisers in his lifetime.

WE RAISED OUR GLASSES TO THE MAN WHOSE NAME IS ON OUR RESTAURANT AND SANG "TAKE ME OUT TO THE BALL GAME."

The Toast took on a life of its own, which seemed appropriate. But when the cocktail waitress told me to call some place in Mexico on that December day in 2001, I have to say I had my reservations.

"I'm not ready to take this whole thing international," I replied. "And besides, I've never even heard of the No Name Café."

She didn't say another word before turning and going back to work. It was as if the thought, or revelation, had been channeled. I'm not sure she ever brought it up again. In fact, I don't even know if she had heard of the No Name Café before the words first came out of her mouth.

The next morning, the first call I received was from Cook County Judge Bill O'Malley, who had been a friend of Harry's. The judge had been in Mexico when Harry died and was unable to make it back to Chicago for the funeral. He later told me of being on the beach when he received word of Harry's death. Instinctively, said Judge O'Malley, he grabbed his glass and headed into the water. Others on the beach, most of them presumably Americans, followed as news of Harry's passing spread from chair to chair, towel to towel. Within minutes the beach had emptied, everyone filing into the water and joining the judge. More than 1,000 miles from Chicago, people who didn't even know one another together raised their glasses and bottles and toasted Harry.

"You have to call the No Name Café in Puerto Vallarta, Mexico," Judge O'Malley told me on the phone.

I was stunned. Two people, completely unconnected, talking about the same place in less than twenty-four hours.

Not five minutes after hanging up the phone with Judge O'Malley, another call came in. This time it was from one of our managers at our Rosemont, Illinois, restaurant.

"Grant, I had a dream last night," she said. "You have to call a place called the No Name Café in Puerto Vallarta, Mexico, and have them toast Harry."

I couldn't believe it. The whole thing was becoming a bit freaky. I walked up three flights of stairs to my office above the restaurant. Three people, completely independent of one another, had told me the exact same thing. I still had no idea what the No Name Café was or if it even existed.

I told my associate, Beth, the story of the three No Name mentions. "Do you think we should call this place?" I asked.

Before Beth could answer, the lights in our offices started flashing on and off repeatedly. We got nervous. Instinctively, I screamed:

"OKAY, HARRY, I WILL CALL THE NO NAME CAFÉ."

The lights immediately stopped flashing.

Two months later the No Name Café played host to the largest crowd ever at one bar to toast Harry: 500 people. In Puerto Vallarta, Mexico!

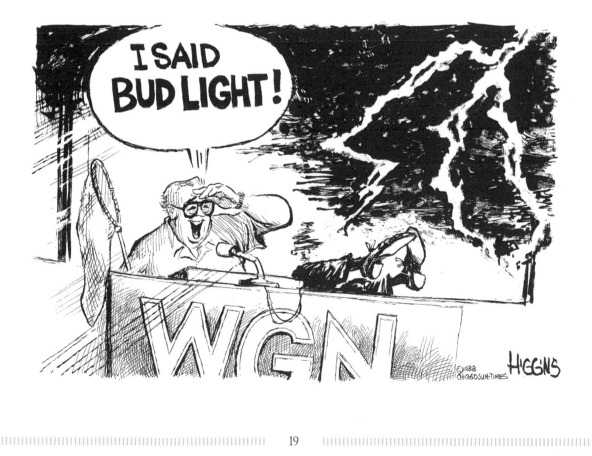

USA TODAY CALLED THE 2002 TOAST TO HARRY AN "INTERNATIONAL PHENOMENON."

A year later, February 21, 2003—the fifth anniversary Toast—300,000 people participated worldwide. Why 300,000? Because that's how many drinks Harry estimated he consumed in his lifetime.

In 2005, Academy Award-winning special effects guru Michael Lantieri, a passionate Cubs fan, took time out during the filming of a *Pirates of the Carribean* movie and used a cannon on the set to shoot a baseball skyward in Harry's honor.

For the tenth anniversary Toast, on February 21, 2008, the restaurant set a Guinness World Record for the largest glass of beer: one hundred gallons. Why one hundred? Because one hundred countries participated in the toast in the one-hundredth year since the Cubs last won the World Series.

But I'm getting ahead of myself. As I said, this tale all started with Harry, but it gathered steam and urgency in 2003 as the Cubs rolled toward the World Series, only to be denied once again. By the time we blew up the Infamous Cubs Foul Ball in 2004, it became clear that the source of the Cubs' World Series drought had to be identified so it could be eliminated.

All signs pointed back into history, well beyond any goat, or at least beyond any goat appearing after 1908. Indeed, all signs pointed to 1908.

Or more to the point, toward one man: Charles W. Murphy, president of the Chicago National League Baseball Club from 1906 to 1913.

What follows is the story of a search that not only exposed Mr. Murphy, but also uncovered Murphy's wayward behavior that led to the greatest and most enduring hoodoo of all time.

GRANT DEPORTER

◉ ◉ ◉

LEADING OFF

In the beginning there was
THE BIG INNING.

Otherwise known as the top of the eighth in Game 6 of the 2003 National League Championship Series.

The Cubs led the Florida Marlins in the best-of-seven series, 3-2, and the final two games were to be played at Wrigley Field. With the Cubs holding a 3-0 lead in Game 6 and needing just five outs for their first World Series appearance since 1945, fate orchestrated yet another cruel intervention.

With one out in the eighth inning, Cubs pitcher Mark Prior was trying to close down a Marlins rally and preserve his three-hit shutout. Juan Pierre stood on second base when Luis Castillo lifted a foul ball toward the left-field line. Cubs left fielder Moises Alou drifted toward the brick wall beyond the bullpen. As the ball floated toward the seats, longtime Cubs fan Steve Bartman and others reached to catch the ball, as virtually any fan would have done. Bartman, seemingly unaware of Alou's presence, got his hands on the ball first, and Alou was unable to make the catch. Alou slammed his glove against the wall in frustration. The Cubs argued for an interference call, but the umpires ruled it was merely a foul ball into the stands.

Given the Cubs history, which almost instantly returned to its familiar rhythm of futility, the team collapsed, and the Marlins roared back to win the game, 8-3. The following night, the Marlins won again and advanced to the World Series instead of the Cubs.

The invisible hand of hoodoo had been extended once again. DePorter knew something wasn't right; A Cubs fan had nothing to do with the team's latest failing. Although others blamed Bartman, DePorter steadfastly refused to fault a poor fan who was in the wrong place at the wrong time.

"From now on we're going to call it the Infamous Cubs Foul Ball—not the Bartman Ball," DePorter declared.

IT HAD TO BE THE BALL'S FAULT.

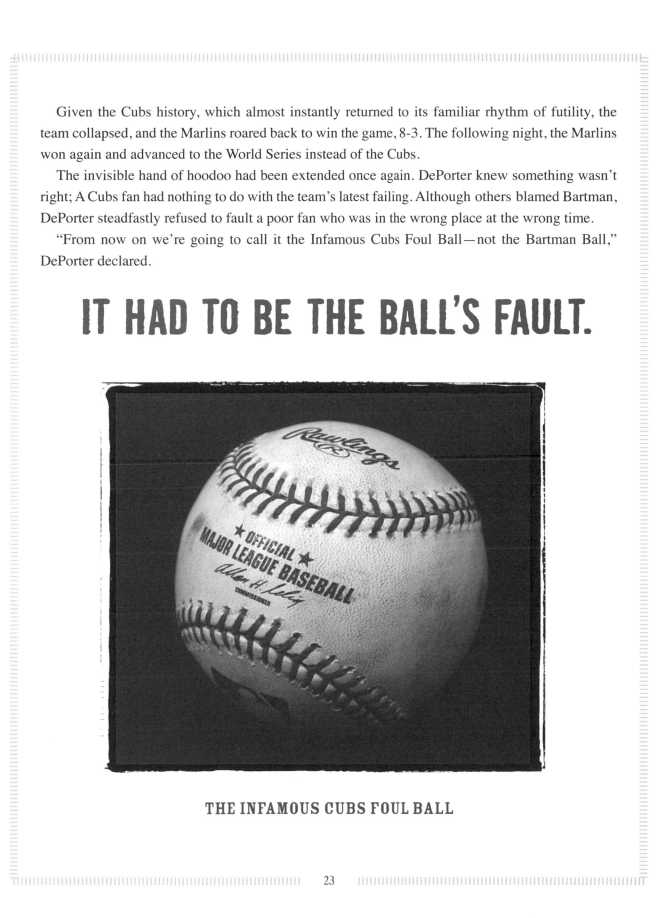

THE INFAMOUS CUBS FOUL BALL

That Bartman didn't even end up with the ball suggested as much. Besides, more than ninety years of unrest had preceded the Infamous Cubs Foul Ball drifting eerily into that October 14 night.

When the opportunity presented itself two months later, DePorter did not hesitate. In the December chill of another icy offseason came news that no Cubs fan could ignore: The Infamous Cubs Foul Ball was going to be sold to the highest bidder. The ball initially was put up for auction anonymously, but eventually it was revealed that Jim Staruck, who was seated behind Bartman, ended up with the ball. Now all Staruck wanted to do was get rid of it.

Nearly two years to the day after he called the No Name Café on behalf of the Toast to Harry Caray, DePorter knew he had to get the ball. A lifelong Cubs fan, DePorter entered the December 2003 MastroNet auction with a singular focus.

> "I had no idea what I would do with the ball or what would happen once I had it," he said. "I didn't even know how high the bidding would go. It was insanity. The longer it went on, the more I wondered whether I was going to have to hock the house. I didn't have a plan, and I didn't have a price. I just knew I had to get that ball."

To be certain he had the winning bid, DePorter stayed up all night. His main competition was comic-book creator Todd McFarlane, who had purchased Mark McGwire's seventieth home-run ball for $3.2 million and Barry Bonds' seventy-third home-run ball for $450,000. McFarlane, who owned six of the ten most expensive baseballs ever sold, dropped out when DePorter topped his $96,000 bid.

"The thing is," DePorter said, "the ball was put out there for any anti-Cubs fan to buy. I couldn't let that happen. Our mission from the outset was to clear Steve Bartman's name. Any fan would have done the same thing. Rather than be angry with any one person, we knew it was more appropriate to be mad at the ball. The ball chose to go in that direction; it had nothing to do with a Cubs fan one way or another. It was the ball. And I knew something had to be done about it."

With the ball safe and secure, the question was: What to do with an object that perpetuated the notion of a cursed franchise?

35¢ IN CHICAGO AND SUBURBS, 50¢ ELSEWHERE   ON THE WEB: WWW.SUNTIMES.COM   HOME DELIVERY: CALL 1-888-848-4637   LATE SPORTS FINAL

CHICAGO SUN-TIMES

O'HARE BACK ON TOP – IN NUMBER OF FLIGHT DELAYS PAGE 6 | SATURDAY, DECEMBER 20, 2003 "TRANQUIL" Forecast: Pages 2, 20 32° | 27°

YES, THIS IS THAT DAMN BALL

OFFICIAL ★ MAJOR LEAGUE BASEBALL
Allan H. Selig
COMMISSIONER

MICHAEL SNEED

The foulest ball in the Cubs' long, frustrating history was purchased at auction for $113,824.16 by owners of Harry Caray's restaurant – and Sneed knows what's going to happen to it
Page 3

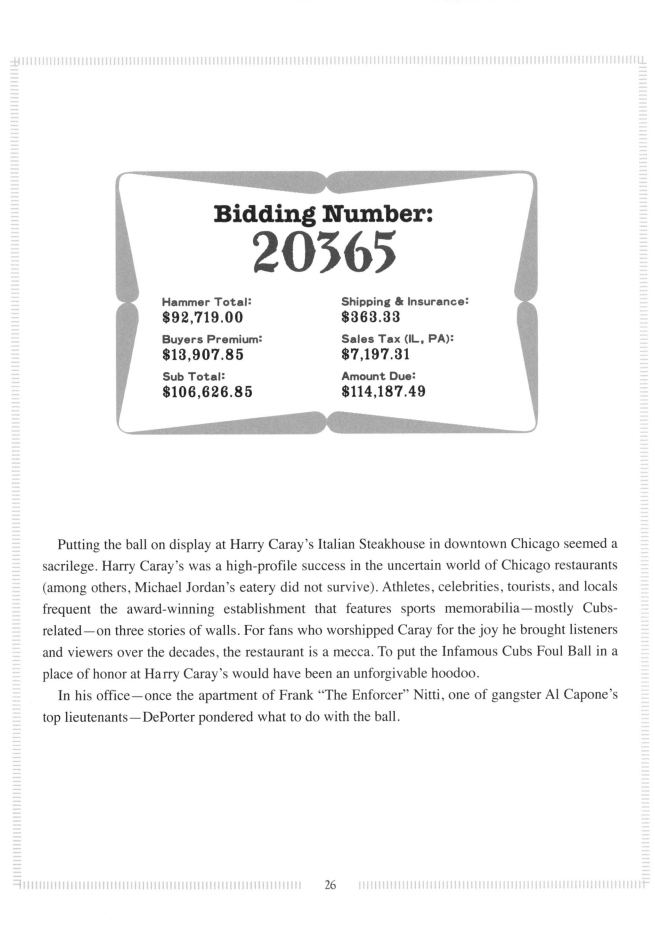

Bidding Number:

20365

Hammer Total:
$92,719.00

Shipping & Insurance:
$363.33

Buyers Premium:
$13,907.85

Sales Tax (IL, PA):
$7,197.31

Sub Total:
$106,626.85

Amount Due:
$114,187.49

Putting the ball on display at Harry Caray's Italian Steakhouse in downtown Chicago seemed a sacrilege. Harry Caray's was a high-profile success in the uncertain world of Chicago restaurants (among others, Michael Jordan's eatery did not survive). Athletes, celebrities, tourists, and locals frequent the award-winning establishment that features sports memorabilia—mostly Cubs-related—on three stories of walls. For fans who worshipped Caray for the joy he brought listeners and viewers over the decades, the restaurant is a mecca. To put the Infamous Cubs Foul Ball in a place of honor at Harry Caray's would have been an unforgivable hoodoo.

In his office—once the apartment of Frank "The Enforcer" Nitti, one of gangster Al Capone's top lieutenants—DePorter pondered what to do with the ball.

IN SHORT ORDER HE KNEW WHAT HAD TO HAPPEN: THE BALL HAD TO BE DESTROYED, AND PERHAPS WITH IT THE HOODOO THAT HAD PLAGUED THE CUBS' ATTEMPTS TO GET TO THE WORLD SERIES. IT WOULD BE A CATHARTIC RELEASE THAT LONG-SUFFERING FANS NEEDED, PARTICULARLY IN THE SHADOWS OF ANOTHER DREARY WINTER.

DePorter called on Cubs fans to help decide how to dispose of the ball. Within a week he received emails, phone calls, and letters in the tens of thousands. Suggestions ranged from launching the ball into outer space to feeding it to a goat. But one theme kept surfacing: Blow up the ball.

Michael Lantieri, an Academy Award-winning special affects guru and a passionate Cubs fan, made an offer that DePorter couldn't refuse. Lantieri offered the use of his state-of-the-art studio and staff to execute a perfect ending for a bad ball.

> *"I have heard you purchased the cursed baseball that kept the Cubs curse alive. I'm a five-time Academy Award-nominated special effects director for motion pictures, and I have some ideas on how to destroy it. As a fan, I would offer my services free, of course. Contact me if you think I can help!!!!!"*

DePorter contacted Lantieri, who had won an Oscar for his work on *Jurassic Park*. They concocted a plan to blow up the ball and whatever nastiness that went along with it.

★ AMONG THE SUGGESTIONS FROM FANS ★

"I can't think of a better way to destroy the ball/curse than having **Bill Murray in full** *Ghostbusters* **gear obliterate it.**" — Chris D., Morris, Illinois

"My suggestion for destroying the ball is to **take a pair of Harry's glasses into the sun and have the reflection burn a hole into the ball.** Harry can have a part in it and help get rid of the curse." — Martha M., Chicago

"I would take the ball to a local steel mill and **throw it in a big ladle full of molten steel.** Drop it from up high from a crane and watch it drop into the liquid steel at 2900 degrees Fahrenheit. It will make a small splash and burn instantly to remove the curse. Other methods, such as liquid nitrogen or grinding it, leave small pieces of the curse floating around. In the liquid steel, it will be completely incinerated, like the *Terminator*." — Larry F., Crown Point, Indiana

"The ball should be cut up so that the Marlins cannot make it a trophy. **It should then be sautéed and fed to a billy goat**—you break two curses all at once." — Jeff K., Wheaton, Illinois

"I hope you'll take the ball and do what Harry would have: **Drown it in Budweiser.**" — Roy R., Arcadia, California

"You have only one choice: The thing must be destroyed. The thing cannot be destroyed by any craft that we here possess. The thing was made in the fires of Mount Doom; only there can it be unmade. **It must be taken deep into Mordor and cast back into the fiery chasm from whence it came.** One of you must do this." — Tony C., Imperial Beach, California

"We live in Bali, a Hindu island, where they hold cleansing ceremonies to rid the world of evil spirits. We suggest that you **burn the ball in a ceremonial cremation pyre** featuring, as appropriate to a Hindu ceremony, a holy cow." — Eliot C., Sanur Bali, Indonesia

"DO NOT DESTROY THE BARTMAN BALL! It should be enshrined and on display in Miami—the home of the Florida Marlins, WORLD SERIES CHAMPIONS!!!!!!!!" — Marlins fan Luciano Cossi, Miami Beach, Florida

"To appease the baseball gods, and as a tribute to Harry, I think the **ball should be sealed in a large container filled with Budweiser and displayed in the restaurant.** If Bud can't fix the curse, nothing will!" — Michael B., East Aurora, New York

"You can't completely destroy the ball because it will only make the curse stronger. What you have to do is **separate the ball into its four main components: leather, yarn, rubber ball, and cork; and then take them to the four corners of the Earth.** That way they'll be separated forever, never to be united again." — Chris L., Chicago

"Sneak into Yankee Stadium under cover of night and bury the ball in center field. **Transfer the curse to the Yankees.**" — Ken, San Francisco

"I have been a loyal Cubs fan for the past twenty years. As you are well aware, our playoff appearances have been few and far between during this period. I remember Bull Durham's mishap at first base in 1984, Will Clark's grand slam in 1989, and the sweep in 1998. However, those all pale in comparison to what occurred on October 14, 2003. That night will be one that will haunt me and all Cub fans forever. I am extremely happy that someone associated with the Chicago Cubs purchased the infamous Bartman Ball, and even happier once I heard your plans for destroying the ball. I truly believe that on February 26, 2004, we will receive some level of closure to that devastating defeat in last year's NLCS. Likewise, I also believe that destroying this ball will be yet another step towards ending the Cubs' World Series drought. Your partnership was forced to pay a handsome fee to ensure that this ball would not be used as fodder against Cubs Nation. To that effect, **I have enclosed a check for five dollars. Please take this and count it**

toward payment of the Bartman Ball. I realize that five dollars is not very much, but it's the symbolization that matters most to me. If you do this, then in some small way I can help participate in bringing closure to a painful night, and hopefully begin a new era in Chicago Cubs baseball. There is no more 'wait till next year.' This year officially begins on February 26. Let us unite and have a New Year's party that will go down in the annals of baseball history." — Dennie D., Winchester, Virginia

*Grind the ball into a fine powder. Then hold a night where the restaurant serves a spaghetti dinner to Cubs fans who pay to attend. The powder is mixed into the spaghetti sauce, and within a day or so the curse would be eliminated. All proceeds could be donated to charity." — Jeff K, Simcoe, Ontario, Canada

"1) Put a hole in it. 2) Put a little bit of black powder in it. 3) Put a five- to seven-inch string in the hole. 4) Light the string, and then KABOOM!!!!!!!!!!!—there's your blown-up baseball. From your nine-year-old exploder." — Kit W., Palm Beach Gardens, Florida

————— Original Message —————
From: Geooklaw
To: holycow@harrycarays.com
Sent: Monday, January 26, 2004 11:42 AM
Subject: Alaska

Hi—

It's not practical for us to get from Douglas Island, Alaska, to your restaurant to participate in the Bartman Ball festivities, so we are holding a parallel party.

On February 26, 2004, at 12:30 pm, we will assemble on the ice of frozen Mendenhall Lake, at the face of Mendenhall Glacier, where we will loft a high fly of a surrogate baseball onto the ice of the glacier. The ball will work its way deep into a crevice, where it will slowly be pulverized, and the dust will be carried into the lake, then Mendenhall River, then out to the Pacific Ocean for burial at sea.

To express our solidarity with all of the principles of expiation and expungement, we will have all our Cubs regalia and icons with us.

Thank you for this global moment in Cubs history.

Greg Cook
Douglas, Alaska

So it was that February 26, 2004, in conjunction with the annual Worldwide Toast to Harry Caray, became last call for the ball.

Media from around the world, including NBC's *Today* show, came to Chicago for live telecasts. *Today* made its first live Chicago appearance in two decades only after DePorter refused to take the ball to New York.

"It belongs to Cubs fans," DePorter said, "and it belongs in Chicago."

Who could disagree?

On its final day, the ball received royal treatment. As noted by *Chicago Sun-Times* **writer Lucio Guerrero, "The only thing missing was a last cigarette."**

Indeed, the ball had a glorious going-out party. With heavy security, the ball was whisked off to Wrigley Field. After circling the fabled ballpark, it was taken to the Amalfi Hotel on Kinzie Street, where it rested on a king-size bed in a fifth-floor suite. A final dinner of lobster, steak, and Budweiser was served, followed by a massage complete with oils and scented candles.

"Oh, Mr. Ball," said massage therapist Cathy Lowman. "I hear you've been in a lot of trouble. I feel a lot of tension. I'm going to give you the maximum care today."

Why a massage?

"The ball is all wound up," Lowman noted. As if this were a laughing matter.

Television trucks lined the streets for blocks. Mayor Richard Daley closed streets in front of the restaurant and rerouted CTA buses to accommodate the crowd that grew throughout the day.

"I have no intention whatsoever of exercising my right to grant clemency or pardon or reprieve," said Illinois governor Rod R. Blagojevich, a lifelong Cubs fan. "THAT BASEBALL HAS GOT TO GO."

At 7:32 p.m., with a group of VIPs gathered in a tent outside, and hundreds of onlookers craning their necks to see, the end of the Infamous Cubs Foul Ball was at hand.

Crowd gathers for the destruction of the ball

"THE BALL BELONGS TO CUBS FANS, AND IT BELONGS IN CHICAGO."

· · · · GRANT DEPORTER · · · ·

TODAY'S LINEUP OF EVENTS

4:00 A.M.: **Kinzie Street blocked off between State and Dearborn**

4:00 P.M.: **Montgomery Street Band performs**

4:48 P.M.: **Wayne Messmer sings the national anthem**

5:04 P.M.: **Harry Caray sound-a-like contest is held**

5:30 P.M.: **Second City troupe performs**

5:41 P.M.: **Joel Murray (brother of Bill) reads "Murray Brothers Proclamation"**

6:00 P.M.: **Harold Ramis, master of ceremonies**

6:15 P.M.: **Alice Peacock performs**

6:35 P.M.: **Billy Corgan and Rick Nielsen perform**

7:31 P.M.: **Dutchie Caray leads the crowd in "Take Me Out to the Ball Game"**

7:32 P.M.: **The ball is destroyed**

7:37 P.M.: **Rev. David Ryan—the Caray family priest—blesses the Cubs 2004 season**

8:00 P.M.: **It's all over**

Grant DePorter

Billy Corgan and Rick Nielsen

Harold Ramis, master of ceremonies

34

A hole was drilled into the ball and explosives were inserted that were so powerful they could have launched pieces of the torn-apart ball at 8,000 feet per second. A flash of lights inside the clear, bulletproof tank where the ball resided was accompanied by three pops and a slow oozing sound.

In six seconds, a force of explosives, heat, and pressure reduced the ball to shreds.

"For the first time in 95 years of curses, hexes and weird symbolism, someone is challenging the evil forces head-on," wrote *Chicago Sun-Times* columnist Jay Mariotti.

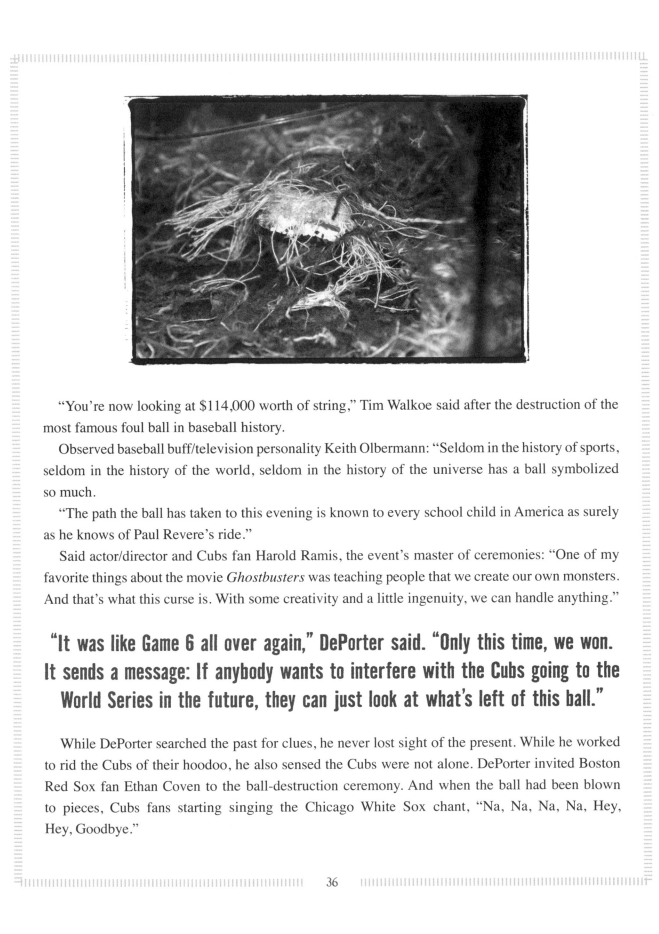

"You're now looking at $114,000 worth of string," Tim Walkoe said after the destruction of the most famous foul ball in baseball history.

Observed baseball buff/television personality Keith Olbermann: "Seldom in the history of sports, seldom in the history of the world, seldom in the history of the universe has a ball symbolized so much.

"The path the ball has taken to this evening is known to every school child in America as surely as he knows of Paul Revere's ride."

Said actor/director and Cubs fan Harold Ramis, the event's master of ceremonies: "One of my favorite things about the movie *Ghostbusters* was teaching people that we create our own monsters. And that's what this curse is. With some creativity and a little ingenuity, we can handle anything."

"It was like Game 6 all over again," DePorter said. "Only this time, we won. It sends a message: If anybody wants to interfere with the Cubs going to the World Series in the future, they can just look at what's left of this ball."

While DePorter searched the past for clues, he never lost sight of the present. While he worked to rid the Cubs of their hoodoo, he also sensed the Cubs were not alone. DePorter invited Boston Red Sox fan Ethan Coven to the ball-destruction ceremony. And when the ball had been blown to pieces, Cubs fans starting singing the Chicago White Sox chant, "Na, Na, Na, Na, Hey, Hey, Goodbye."

"A lot of people, myself included, thought we had to get the Red Sox out of the way first," DePorter said. "Then we had to do the same with the White Sox. Now it is undisputable that when we win the World Series it will the biggest moment in sports history."

To that end, DePorter graciously sent pieces of the blown-apart Infamous Cubs Foul Ball to Boston in July 2004, where former Harry Caray's Restaurant Group marketing director Beth Goldberg Heller had moved. She took pieces of the ball to Fenway Park, and as part of a curse-ending ritual, Goldberg Heller sang "Take Me Out to the Ball Game" before sprinkling the ball shreds on the outfield grass.

As the 2004 postseason got underway, DePorter and his staff hung a six-foot sign in the entrance to the restaurant. The sign read:

"Good luck, Red Sox. Prove Curses Don't Exist."

That was an idea Cubs fans could embrace. In fact, so many of them signed the large sign that it turned into a sea of black ink. Just to be certain the curse-busting spirits were aligned, the restaurant served Boston-style food throughout the playoffs.

On June 3, 2005, DePorter and his staff took pieces of the Infamous Cubs Foul Ball to U.S. Cellular Field, home of the White Sox, where they repeated the ritual carried out a year earlier in Boston. Holding pieces of the ball, they sang "Take Me Out to the Ball Game," and then a member of Harry Caray's Restaurant Group threw out the ceremonial first pitch.

Grant and Joanna DePorter, Ethan Coven

As if on cue, the White Sox did their part. Not only did they exorcize their hoodoo, they became the second team in history to win their last eight games of the season. The first team was the 2004 Red Sox.

Meanwhile, remains of the ball also were taken to Wrigley Field.

DePorter knew that whatever the nature of the curse, hex, hoodoo, or bad omen, it could not be reversed or eliminated in a single act. The Infamous Cubs Foul Ball had not only unceremoniously disrupted one life, that of Bartman, but it had done so in an eerily familiar way. There had to be more to the story, DePorter thought.

TASTE OF CHICAGO

The ball was gone, but the Cubs' continued failure to win the World Series frustrated their fans.

"At the urging of faithful Cubs fans, Harry Caray's will try once again to use the power of the ball to generate positive energy for the Cubs," DePorter said in 2005. Drawing on ideas originally submitted by several fans, DePorter cooked up a palatable solution: Eat it.

Once again, in an effort to leave nothing to chance with another curse-busting effort, DePorter assembled a team of experts:

EBERHARD ZWERGEL – Senior Lecturer in Chemistry at Northwestern University

GRETCHEN VERDOON – Prominent microbiologist

KRISTA WENNERSTROM – Nutritionist from Thorek Memorial Hospital (Wrigley Field neighbor)

DAVID HARTER – Curse-buster from Sports Curse Laboratory, a Boston-based company specializing in the prevention, detection, and elimination of sports curses

All that remained was for experts to chew on the concept and come up with something digestible. Ultimately it was determined that the "essence of the ball" could be extracted by distilling a solution containing ball fibers.

"Once all the leather and the rubber were removed, we were left with natural fibers," Wennerstrom said.

The fibers went into a large container of Budweiser, vodka, bay leaves, oregano, rosemary, and thyme.

"We boiled it, then it went through a distilling and purifying process," said Wennerstrom, a Cubs fan.

The process produced almost a gallon of liquid.

Sports Curse Laboratories
13 Industrial Park
Boston, MA. 02127
800-NOCURSE

Friday, February 25, 2005

Mr Grant DePorter
Harry Caray's Restaurant
33 West Kinzie
Chicago, IL 60610

Our Chicago Branch Lab has completed sample testing from the Steve Bartman ball under the auspices of our representatives, Leigh and David Harter Ph.Ds. We used DNA based PCR (polymerase chain reaction) methods on samples before and after your curse-ending experiment at Harry Carry's Restaurant. This method was scientifically validated here in our Boston lab, resulting in the success of the 2004 World Champion Red Sox.

From the DNA diagram below we have diagnosed that curse conditions exist in the sample we tested before your curse ending experiment.

However, we see no evidence of this condition from the second sample taken after the curse-ending event. As you can see from the DNA example below, it has clearly disappeared.

This leads us to the firm conclusion that your curse ending experiment was a success and the Steve Bartman Ball Curse no longer affects the Chicago Cubs Major League Baseball team. We are sure all die-hard Cub fans will sincerely appreciate your efforts to help your team bring home a World Championship.

Dr. Michael Evans, MD, Ph.D. – Technical Director (Boston)

Dr. Bobbi Evans, Ph.D. – General Manager (Boston)

Sports Curse Detection, Elimination and Prevention

"It was essentially like holy water then," DePorter said. "It had a nice smell to it. So we transferred that into our marinara sauce."

The curse-breaking sauce was served for four days to 700 patrons leading up to the 2005 Annual Worldwide Toast to Harry Caray. Patrons paid $11.95 to take a bite out of the curse, with proceeds going to the Juvenile Diabetes Research Foundation.

"I'm afraid Grant took the phrase, 'Everybody likes a good baseball yarn' too literally," said *Chicago Tribune* food critic Phil Vettel. "I'm not sure what a baseball tastes like, or what string tastes like, or what a reversed curse tastes like. They probably taste like chicken though."

Grant DePorter

"IT WAS ESSENTIALLY LIKE HOLY WATER. IT HAD A NICE SMELL TO IT. SO WE TRANSFERRED THAT INTO OUR MARINARA SAUCE."

GRANT DEPORTER
ON DISTILLING THE INFAMOUS CUBS FOUL BALL

⊙ ⊙ ⊙ ⊙

THE PAPER TRAIL

With the Cubs' hoodoo showing no sign of abating in 2005, DePorter dived into history. A friend brought over an entire collection of Chicago newspapers from 1908. Every page of the *Chicago American, Daily News, Record-Herald*, and *Tribune*, piled high into a four-foot mountain of information. Add in a year's worth of *Sporting Life* magazines that DePorter found and devoured, and he estimated that he read more than a million words, all the while looking for clues.

The 1908 newspaper pages were so brittle that tiny pieces broke off every time DePorter turned a page. Taking great care, DePorter gently slid the pages as he moved from one to another, not sure what he was looking for, but certain that the pile of one-hundred-year-old newsprint held some answers.

Along the way, DePorter found nuggets on Chicago life in 1908. More often than not, these finds were buried in long stories or appeared as an item so unadorned that it seemed an afterthought. He saw ads that claimed beer was a health product necessary for every man and woman of drinking age. He came across an article promoting animal-to-human spine transplants.

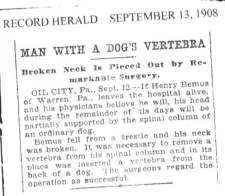

RECORD HERALD   SEPTEMBER 13, 1908

MAN WITH A DOG'S VERTEBRA

Broken Neck Is Pieced Out by Remarkable Surgery.

OIL CITY, Pa., Sept. 12.--If Henry Bemus of Warren, Pa., leaves the hospital alive, and his physicians believe he will, his head during the remainder of his days will be partially supported by the spinal column of an ordinary dog.

Bemus fell from a trestle and his neck was broken. It was necessary to remove a vertebra from his spinal column and in its place was inserted a vertebra from the back of a dog. The surgeons regard the operation as successful.

DePorter perused the papers several hours each night after returning home from work. Delving into 1908 became

an almost obsessive hobby. His wife and children thought the endeavor bordered on the eccentric, but they overcame their skepticism to appreciate his crusade.

When pouring over the papers for clues to the mystery of the hoodoo, DePorter wore a bandana over his face as a dust mask. The papers were so brittle that tiny fibers broke off the pages, causing everyone nearby to sneeze.

Had DePorter been conducting his research in a traditional academic setting, you might have thought he was working on his Ph.D. But he was on to something.

AND THEN ONE NIGHT—EUREKA!

CHICAGO DAY.

Oct. 9, 1871—When the cow kicked over the lamp.

Oct. 9, 1908—When the Cubs kicked over the Giants.

It didn't take long for DePorter to know he had stumbled upon the source of whatever hoodoo vexed the Cubs. Somewhere in all the worn-out newspaper pages and the hundreds of hours spent researching every nub of a clue, the answer would be found in 1908.

CHICAGO DAILY NEWS   SEPTEMBER 19, 1908

TRAPPED BY FLAME IN FIGHT TO SAVE SQUARE

Many Buildings in Danger as Fire Sweeps Through Structures at 651 West Van Buren Street and 240 Wood.

By 1908 Chicago had grown up and out of the ashes of the great fire of 1871 into one of the world's most vibrant cities, teeming with more than two million people. The Chicago stockyards were world renown, and the city's architecture and industry rivaled that of New York.

As much as anything, Chicago meant baseball. The game revolved around the city to a degree unimaginable in 2008. It was a different time, to be sure—White Sox owner Charles Comiskey actually said that if his team didn't get to the World Series, he would cheer for the Cubs to make it.

Two years earlier, the Cubs had won a National League-record 116 games in a 154-game season. Meanwhile, Comiskey, as shrewd a practitioner of hoodoo as any owner in baseball, had purchased what became known as the Hoodoo Hen, a bird credited with helping the White Sox stun the Cubs and win the World Series. Few could have imagined a scenario in which Comiskey's "Hitless Wonders," as the White Sox were known in 1906, would even come close to beating the mighty Cubs.

After the Cubs beat the Detroit Tigers in the 1907 World Series, the prevailing opinion was that they might be too good for baseball. League executives went so far as to admit, as reported in the *Chicago Daily News*, that baseball would be better off if victories were spread around a little more democratically. Some called it the "good of the league policy."

CUBS WORRY THE HOODOO MAN.

Marooned.

"Because the Cubs were so dominant going into the 1908 season, the board of the National League believed that for the 'good of the league' the team needed to be handicapped," the *Daily News* reported. "Rules were unbalanced. When umpires made their calls, the benefit of the doubt always went to the other team."

Poring over thousands of pages of old newspapers provided DePorter with a unique insight into the era that would lead him to a stunning discovery. His "field notes," as they were, began to organize in at least three clusters. First, the fans were critical to the Cubs' success in 1908. The West Side Rooters Social Club had organized that year, with Cubs players and manager Frank Chance taking leadership roles in the group, much to owner Charles W. Murphy's disgust. Second, hoodoo and all its implications on and off the field, had as much to do with the baseball experience as the game itself. Finally, it became clear to DePorter that the Cubs overcame a formidable list of obstacles, real and imagined, to win the 1908 championship.

Superstition has always been a part of sport, particularly with its participants, but it was never more apparent than in 1908. Hoodoos were common editorial fodder for writers in every section of the paper. The *New York Times* had a front-page story about the ubiquitous nature of superstitions in all walks of life throughout the country. The *Chicago Tribune* addressed hoodoos in an editorial. Cartoonists for all four major Chicago newspapers referred to hoodoos almost daily. For Chicago baseball writers, hoodoos were as much a part of the game as fly balls and double plays.

Hoodoos were taken so seriously that New York Highlanders manager Clark Griffith voluntarily resigned in late June 1908. According to a *Tribune* account, "The circumstances surrounding the withdrawal of Griffith from the Highlanders are unparalleled in baseball. He quit because he thought he was unlucky, and that [owner] Frank Farrell might have a change in his baseball fortunes if a new man was in charge."

Beyond that, DePorter noticed an eerie symmetry between the years 1908 and 2008. To wit:

*

The great banking crisis of 1907 adversely affected the U.S. economy. In 1908 the country continued to struggle economically due to the financial fallout.

*

The U.S. presidential candidates in both 1908 and 2008 sought to replace a Republican in the White House.

*

Oil news bubbled up from the Middle East.

*

The 1908 Summer Olympics were in London, the world's dominant economic power, and the 2008 Olympics were in China, an emerging world power.

*

Early-season monsoon-like rains washed out an unprecedented number of baseball games.

MY WORD HOW RIPPING

BAH JOVE AINT IT JOLLY

BRITISH ROOTERS AT THE OLYMPIAD WHEN THEY WON SOMETHING YESTERDAY.

Cub Tracks Made with Fore Paws as Found on Contracts in Masonic Temple Safe.

To appreciate the grand scale of the Cubs' 1908 production, it is important to know the cast of characters.

THE MANAGER

◦ FRANK CHANCE ◦

Nicknamed "The Peerless Leader," Chance also played first base. He replaced an ill Frank Selee as manager on July 1, 1905. From 1906 to 1910, Chance led the Cubs to four pennants and two World Series championships. Also nicknamed "Husk" because of his powerful six-foot, 190-pound frame, Chance started out as a catcher until Selee moved him to first base, a change that enabled Chance to become part of the "Tinkers to Evers to Chance" double-play combination immortalized by Franklin P. Adams in 1910. Chance might have been even more gifted with his fists.

"You do things my way," he told his players, "or you meet me after the game."

Chance was quick to instigate an altercation if he thought it necessary, such as throwing bottles tossed onto the field by fans right back at them. In 1907, Chance did just that in Brooklyn, and a young boy suffered a cut on his leg. Mobbed by angry fans, Chance departed the park under police escort. Chance was a fierce competitor—he fined players ten dollars for shaking hands with an opponent. Chance was as defiant as he was tough. He stood as close to the plate as possible when batting, and was beaned by pitches so often that his hearing was impaired. From Chance's perspective, playing poker helped keep a player's mind sharp, though his games had a twenty-five-cent limit. He also believed betting on horses was therapeutic. After demanding intensity on

BASE BALL, TRAP SHOOTING AND GENERAL SPORTS

Title Registered in U. S. Patent Office.

Vol. 52—No. 7   Philadelphia, October 24, 1908   Price 5 Cents

REULBACH, P.   M. BROWN, P.   LUNDGREN, P.   OVERALL, P.   FRASER, P.

COAKLEY P.   KLING C.

PFEISTER, P.   MORAN, C.

CHICAGO BASE BALL CLUB OF NATIONAL LEAGUE 1908

FRANK CHANCE MGR. & 1ST. B.

CHAMPIONS FOR 1908

ALSO CHAMPIONS OF THE WORLD

EVERS, 2D. B.   STEINFELDT, 3D. B.   TINKER, S.S.   HOFMAN, UTILITY

ZIMMERMAN, UTILITY.   HOWARD, UTILITY.   SHECKARD O.F.   SLAGLE, O.F.   SCHULTE, O.F.

Sporting Life
PHILADELPHIA.

the field, he helped his players unwind by buying them beer after home games at a saloon across the street from the ballpark. Among Chance's great contributions was making sure the Chicago National League club forever was known as the "Cubs."

◦ JOHNNY EVERS ◦

Second baseman: Scrawny, scrappy, and high-strung, Evers batted left-handed and was known as "The Crab." Some say it was for his defensive stance; others say it was for his disposition.

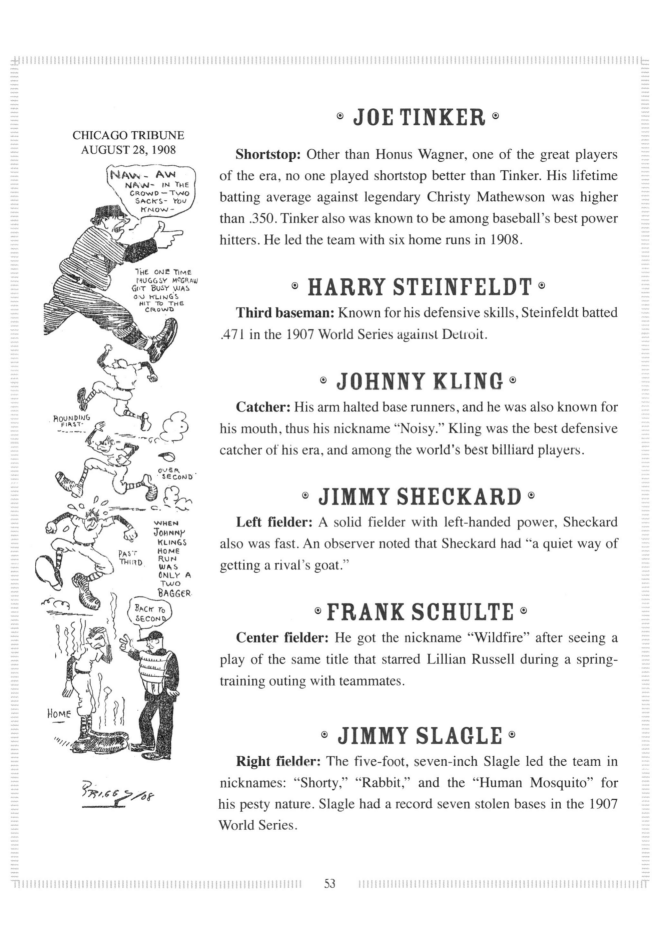

NAW- AW NAW- IN THE CROWD—TWO SACKS- YOU KNOW-

THE ONE TIME MUGGSY McGRAW GOT BUSY WAS ON KLINGS HIT TO THE CROWD

ROUNDING FIRST-

OVER SECOND

PAST THIRD.

WHEN JOHNNY KLINGS HOME RUN WAS ONLY A TWO BAGGER.

BACK TO SECOND

HOME

BRIGGS/08

◦ JOE TINKER ◦

Shortstop: Other than Honus Wagner, one of the great players of the era, no one played shortstop better than Tinker. His lifetime batting average against legendary Christy Mathewson was higher than .350. Tinker also was known to be among baseball's best power hitters. He led the team with six home runs in 1908.

◦ HARRY STEINFELDT ◦

Third baseman: Known for his defensive skills, Steinfeldt batted .471 in the 1907 World Series against Detroit.

◦ JOHNNY KLING ◦

Catcher: His arm halted base runners, and he was also known for his mouth, thus his nickname "Noisy." Kling was the best defensive catcher of his era, and among the world's best billiard players.

◦ JIMMY SHECKARD ◦

Left fielder: A solid fielder with left-handed power, Sheckard also was fast. An observer noted that Sheckard had "a quiet way of getting a rival's goat."

◦ FRANK SCHULTE ◦

Center fielder: He got the nickname "Wildfire" after seeing a play of the same title that starred Lillian Russell during a spring-training outing with teammates.

◦ JIMMY SLAGLE ◦

Right fielder: The five-foot, seven-inch Slagle led the team in nicknames: "Shorty," "Rabbit," and the "Human Mosquito" for his pesty nature. Slagle had a record seven stolen bases in the 1907 World Series.

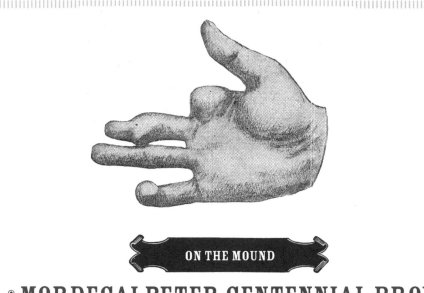

◦ MORDECAI PETER CENTENNIAL BROWN ◦

Right-hander: A childhood accident involving a piece of farm equipment cost Brown much of his right index finger. Sportswriters no doubt figured "Three-and-a-Fraction Finger" Brown was a bit too wordy, so they settled on "Three Finger" Brown. For Cubs fans still lamenting the Lou Brock trade, consider this: St. Louis dealt Brown to the Cubs for the forgettable duo of pitcher Jack Taylor and catcher Larry McLean. And the Cardinals were in last place when they made the deal.

THE CHICAGO DAILY TRIBUNE   OCTOBER 14, 1908

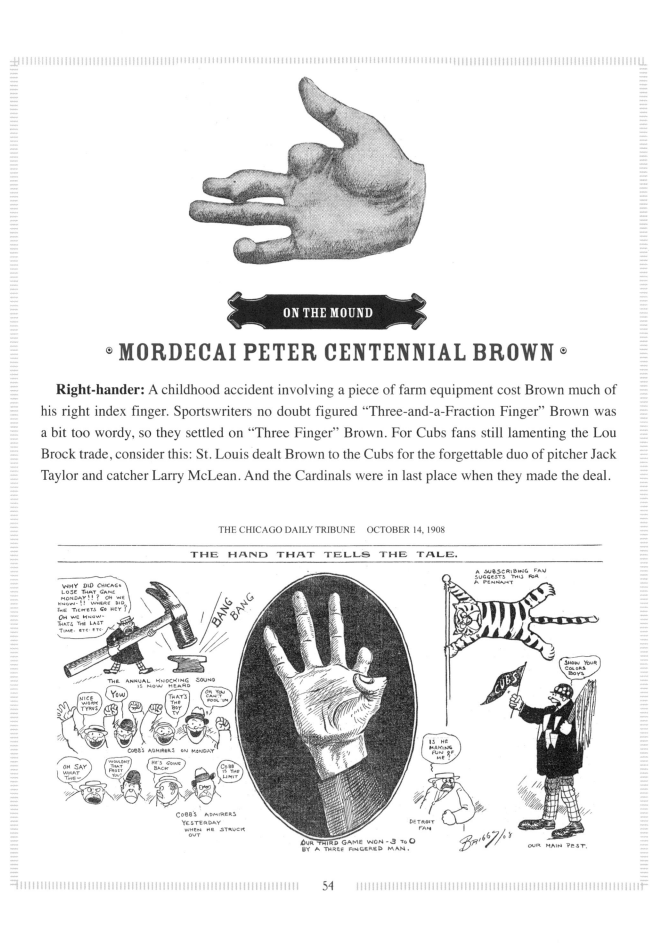

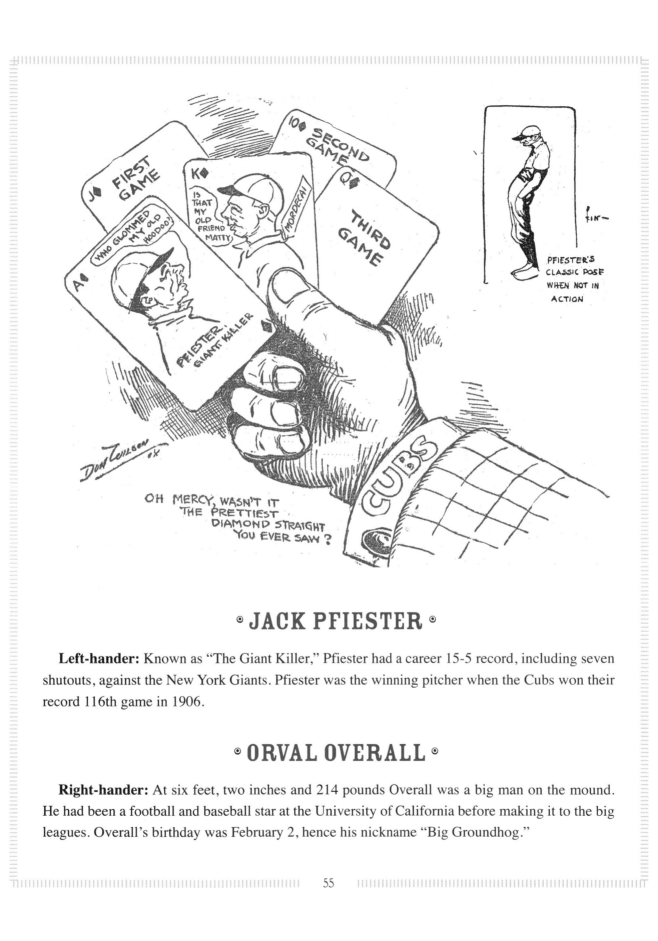

◉ JACK PFIESTER ◉

Left-hander: Known as "The Giant Killer," Pfiester had a career 15-5 record, including seven shutouts, against the New York Giants. Pfiester was the winning pitcher when the Cubs won their record 116th game in 1906.

◉ ORVAL OVERALL ◉

Right-hander: At six feet, two inches and 214 pounds Overall was a big man on the mound. He had been a football and baseball star at the University of California before making it to the big leagues. Overall's birthday was February 2, hence his nickname "Big Groundhog."

⊙ ED REULBACH ⊙

Right-hander: Reulbach had eyesight as poor as his arm was great. His vision was so bad that Cubs catchers painted their gloves white when he was on the mound. Reulbach set a league record with a forty-four-inning scoreless streak in 1908, which was his only twenty-win season.

⊙ CHARLES FRASER ⊙

Right-hander: Fraser never ceased to get the attention of batters. He ranks second all-time in hit batsmen with 219. Fraser had four twenty-loss seasons and two twenty-win seasons, none of either with the Cubs.

⊙ CARL LUNDGREN ⊙

Right-hander: A University of Illinois graduate, Lundgren won ten consecutive games against the Boston Doves over four seasons. He had the only sub-.500 record (6-9) on the 1908 team.

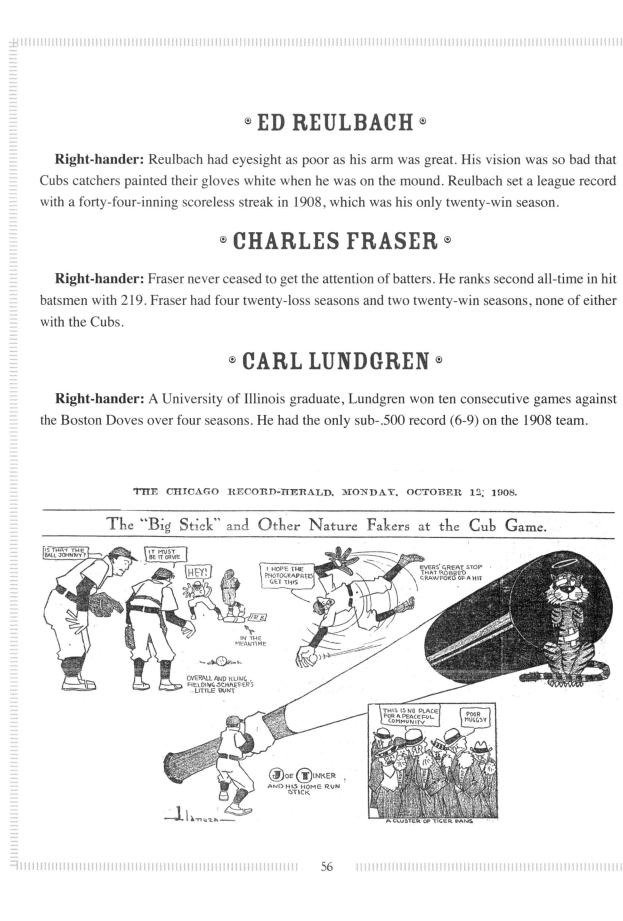

THE CHICAGO RECORD-HERALD, MONDAY, OCTOBER 12, 1908.

⊙ ARTIE HOFMAN ⊙ ⊙

Outfielder/infielder: Fleet-footed jolly "Solly" was also known as "Circus Solly," though it wasn't clear whether he acquired the nickname for his circus catches or after a cartoon character of the era.

⊙ HEINIE ZIMMERMAN ⊙

Infielder/outfielder: He was known as an excellent bad-ball hitter. Zimmerman often referred to himself in the third person.

⊙ DEL HOWARD ⊙

Outfielder/infielder: A starter for other teams, he was not good enough to play regularly for the Cubs. Howard's only home run of the season helped the Cubs to a seventeen-inning tie with the Boston Doves.

⊙ PAT MORAN ⊙

Catcher: A valuable veteran, Moran filled in when Kling suffered a broken thumb. He later managed Cincinnati to the 1919 World Series championship over the scandalized Chicago White Sox.

⊙ ⊙ ⊙ ⊙ ⊙ ⊙ ⊙ ⊙ ⊙ ⊙ ⊙ ⊙ ⊙ ⊙ ⊙

At least one other character emerged in 1908 that deserves more than a mere mention.

DePorter knew he had to continue digging deep into the history of 1908 when he came across the first goat story. As a Cubs fan, DePorter knew about the alleged curse that William "Billy" Sianis put on the Cubs when his goat was denied entry into Wrigley Field during the 1945 World Series. When Sianis's nephew, Sam Sianis, owner of Chicago's iconic Billy Goat Tavern, later brought a goat to Wrigley to reverse his uncle's curse, the Cubs continued to lose, and the theory lost some of its kick.

In fact, whatever goat-related hoodoo existed, its roots could be traced back to 1908, when the first goat was turned away by the Cubs for a game at West Side Grounds.

That is the goat in the article that DePorter found in the August 31, 1908, edition of the *Chicago Tribune*. First, a little historical context:

The phrase "get your goat," meaning to annoy, appeared in print for the first time in 1908.

On October 6, 1945, Cubs owner P.K. Wrigley refused entry to Game 4 of the World Series to a goat owned by William Sianis, who had two box seat tickets—at a cost of $7.50 each—for himself and his goat named Murphy. The Cubs had won two of the first three games against the Detroit Tigers. The exchange between Wrigley and Sianis went like this:

WRIGLEY: *"Let Billy in, but not the goat."*

SIANIS: *"Why not the goat?"*

WRIGLEY: *"Because he stinks."*

SIANIS: *"The Cubs ain't gonna win no more. The Cubs will never win a World Series so long as the goat is not allowed in Wrigley Field."*

After the Cubs lost the fourth, fifth, and seventh games at home, Sianis sent a telegram to Wrigley:

"WHO STINKS NOW?"

1973

Chicago Tribune columnist Dave Condon tried to broker a peace by bringing Socrates, a Murphy descendant, to Wrigley Field on July 4. "All is forgiven. Let me lead the Cubs to the pennant," read a sign hanging from the neck of Socrates. " The goat wasn't allowed in the park.

1984

The Cubs took a 2-0 lead in the best-of-five National League Championship Series. Sam Sianis and his goat had been Opening Day guests of the Cubs. After the goat was allowed onto the field, Sam declared, "The curse is lifted." Not quite. The Cubs were eight outs away from the World Series when a ground ball went through the legs of first baseman Leon Durham. The error enabled San Diego to tie the score, and the Padres went on to win the game and advance to the Series.

1989

Sam Sianis and the goat again were on the field for Opening Day. As they had in 1984, the Cubs won their division. The goat stayed home during the playoffs, and the Cubs lost to San Francisco.

1994

With the Cubs mired in a twelve-game home losing streak, Sam and the goat tried to change the team's fortunes. They were initially rebuffed, but Ernie Banks escorted them back into the park. The Cubs won, 5-2, breaking the skid.

1998

Sam and the goat were in attendance as the Cubs defeated San Francisco in a one-game playoff for the National League wild card. The Cubs had ninety victories entering the playoffs in the ninetieth year since their last World Series. The goat stayed home, and the Cubs lost to Atlanta in the division series.

The point of this history lesson, as DePorter discovered, is that any goat-related hoodoo clearly originated in 1908.

On June 19, 1908 the following headline and story appeared in the *Tribune*:

"THIS MASCOT IS UNLUCKY: CUSTOMS MEN BAR A GOAT

Chicago customs agents twice denied entry to a large Rocky Mountain billy goat that had traveled a reported 2,400 miles.

"Unless the Excelsior sails to another country than the United States or Cuba, the goat will have to spend the remainder of its existence aboard the ship unless killed or compelled to walk the plank."

But the real story involved a goat taken to the Cubs home park and then escorted out:

"One happy rooter proudly escorted a diminutive goat off the field of battle after it was over under the impression it would be accorded the place now occupied by Schulte's bull pup as mascot," reported the *Tribune* on August 31, 1908.

Now it's one thing to discover that a goat was rejected by the Cubs in 1908. It's of an entirely different magnitude when you consider that finding alongside a cartoon depicting a member of the "Goat Club," which was founded in 1908. The man on the lower right, who is with a goat speaking the word "never," looks exactly the way a cartoonist would depict Sam Sianis.

"When I saw the story I was intrigued," DePorter said. "But when I saw the cartoon and the rendering of a man who looks exactly like Sam, I couldn't believe it."

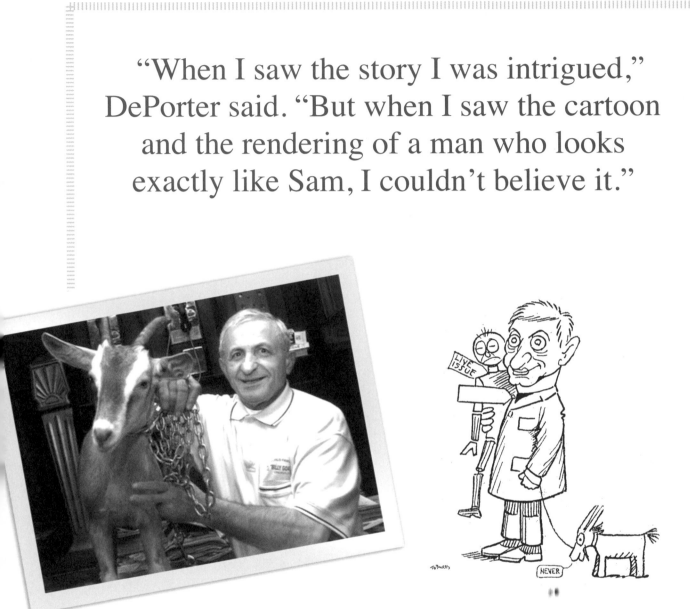

Whatever the nature of the hoodoo that afflicted the Cubs, DePorter knew it had nothing to do with the team or its fans. If you can overcome a goat hoodoo and the National League conjuring up something called "for the good of the game policy," which effectively called for the Cubs' demise, a team can handle whatever comes its way.

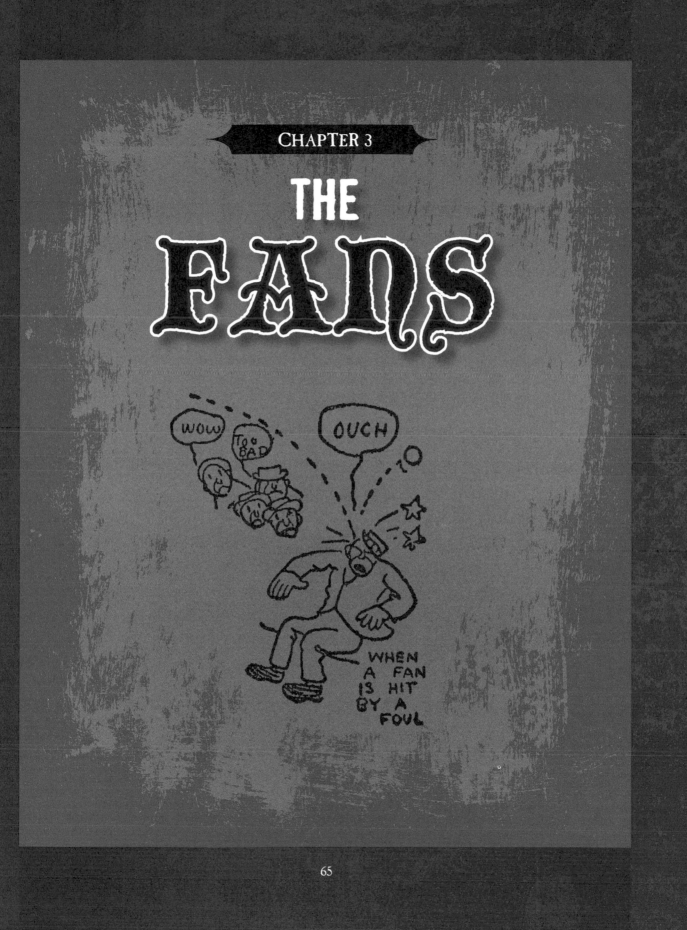

⊙ ⊙ ⊙ ⊙ ⊙ ⊙ ⊙

"If the Sox cannot win first honors in the game, my next best wish is for the Cubs to land them and keep them in Chicago."

WHITE SOX OWNER CHARLES COMISKEY, FEBRUARY 19, 1908

⊙ ⊙ ⊙ ⊙ ⊙ ⊙ ⊙

WHO'S GOING FIRST?

PULLING FOR THE HOME FOLK.

There is no greater ritual in sports than the cheering of an adoring crowd, just as there is nothing more sacred to a franchise than the fans that orchestrate it all.

Oddly, if not ironically, the one person who might have quibbled with the above was Cubs owner Charles W. Murphy, though the depth of his disdain for "scientific rooting," as the West Side Rooters Social Club called it, wouldn't be known until after the 1908 season.

These were strange days indeed for Chicago baseball fans. Fans of the Cubs and White Sox not only got along, they cheered for one another. They also exhibited behavior that might suggest insanity. Fans were so intensively involved in their teams that officials in New York and Chicago feared suicide rates would rise if the teams did not meet expectations. A Cubs fan unable to get into the ballpark, climbed to the top of a rooftop beyond the outfield, only to fall to his death.

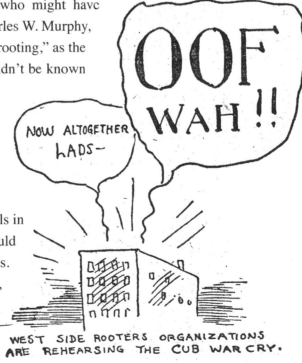

WEST SIDE ROOTERS ORGANIZATIONS ARE REHEARSING THE CUB WAR CRY.

Only Chairs for Two.

THE CHICAGO DAILY NEWS.

FRIDAY, JULY 24, 1908.

THE STEADY CUSTOMER AT THE BALL PARK.

WONDER
WHAT BAN
HAS GOT!

MURPHY

A story in the *Sporting Life* magazine suggested that fans were behaving as if they were going crazy:

"Bugs* have become wild maniacs. The streets are full of wild-eyed bugs, and the strain threatens to over-populate the Illinois asylums. Dense masses of fans gather round every spot where a bulletin can be read, each 'sporting extra' of the evening papers is snapped up with a mad avidity, and the avalanche of 'What's the score?' requests coming over the phones of every newspaper office is enough to ruin the patience of the late Job. Chicago has gone baseball mad."

*A COMMONLY USED TERM FOR FANS IN 1908.

From a fan's perspective, or a player's, for that matter, 1908 was a wholly unique experience. The West Side Rooters Social Club was organized in early 1908 with Chicago attorney Tom Johnson as president of the group. Cubs manager Frank Chance joined the effort, and shortstop Joe Tinker also took a leadership role in the organization.

A report in the *Chicago Tribune*, January 18, 1908:

"One hundred West Side Rooters attended a meeting last night in the People's theater lodge room and organized the West Side Rooters Social Club. Shortstop Joe Tinker was the moving spirit in its formation. The purpose of the organization is to give winter entertainments, and one of the main objects will be to let the south and north sides know that there is a considerable section of the city lying adjacent to the Cubs' ball park."

The group did not have an official affiliation with the Cubs, and something less than Murphy's whole-hearted support.

"I do not see why merchants should donate champagne or edibles to the West Side Rooters Social Club for a social function," Murphy told the *Daily News* in March. "Neither am I able to figure out why Joe Tinker should hand in a ten-dollar bill at the White Sox Rooters Association Ball for a round of lemonade and be given back no change. I am not pessimistic about these clubs and shall do all I can to encourage them, so long as they deserve it."

Tinker explained it to the *Daily News*:

"The way I came to pay ten dollars for the club was this: President [Charles] Comiskey was present and ordered drinks and drank to the health of Frank Chance. It was then up to me as the only member of the Cubs present to return the compliment. I did so and bought drinks for 160 persons and we drank to Comiskey's health."

To understand the influence of the West Side Rooters Social Club, consider that more than 1,000 people attended its first annual ball, in April 1908.

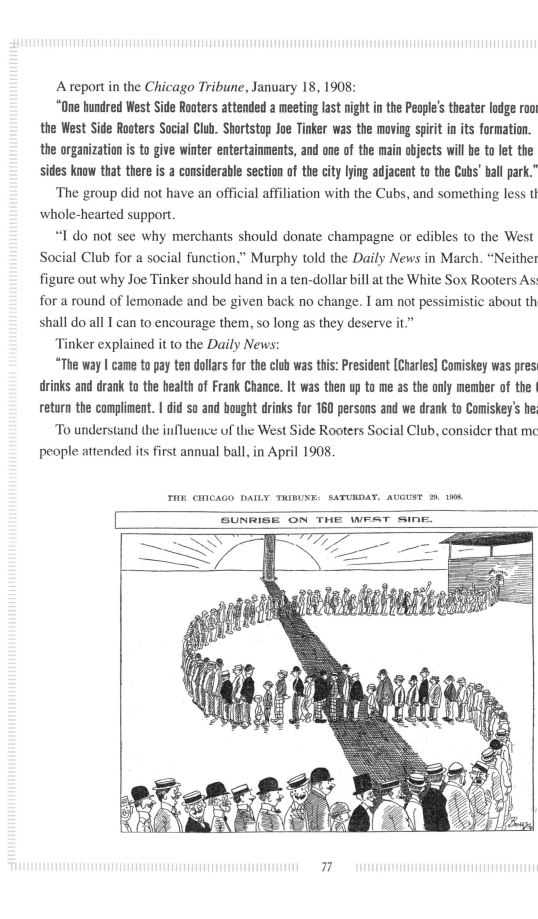

THE CHICAGO DAILY TRIBUNE: SATURDAY, AUGUST 29. 1908.

SUNRISE ON THE WEST SIDE.

The Rooters introduced a new form of cheering, borrowed from college football fans, according to a *Chicago Tribune* editorial.

THEY CALLED IT "SCIENTIFIC ROOTING,"

a more raucous form of support. That anyone, including Murphy, took exception to exuberant fans was peculiar. Prior to the Rooters, it wasn't uncommon for bottles, rocks, and seat cushions to be thrown at players during games. Fights between players and fans, who routinely poured onto the field the minute a game ended, were common, too.

Under the circumstances, it was probably a wise decision to prohibit fans from keeping foul balls, though it no doubt irritated them. Teams employed workers to retrieve foul balls so they could be returned to play.

Murphy certainly wanted spectators at his West Side Grounds, but he clearly had little affinity for the West Side Rooters and seemed chafed that his manager and star shortstop were part of the group.

Here too, DePorter made a discovery that proved prescient. Boston's Royal Rooters, the precursor to Red Sox Nation, helped the team win its first World Series title, in 1903. Trailing Pittsburgh, 3-1, in the best-of-nine series, Boston won four straight, thanks in part to the Royal Rooters singing tunes designed to annoy opposing players. When Boston won again in 1918, the Royal Rooters disbanded, and the Red Sox didn't win another World Series until the Rooters reformed during the 2004 season.

Murphy effectively disbanded the West Side Rooters following the 1908 season. A hoodoo? In DePorter's mind, a damning piece of circumstantial evidence and a part of the hoodoo that afflicted the Cubs through the 2007 season.

The following stories and images provide additional insight into life as a Cubs fan in 1908.

THE CHICAGO DAILY NEWS
MARCH 2, 1908

SPORTING EXTRA
FOR ADDITIONAL SPORTING NEWS SEE PAGE 1 OF THE MAIN SHEET.

TINKER AND BOSS CLASH

Cub Shortstop Seeks Explanation from President
Murphy for Attack on Rooters' Clubs
and Gets It.

"No One Connected with Our Organization Ever Asked Money
from World's Champions," Says Player, but
Fans Object to Levy.

THE CHICAGO DAILY TRIBUNE:
MONDAY, MARCH 2, 1908.

ROOTERS' CLUBS
HIT BY MURPHY.

President of Cubs Warns
Against Danger of Too
Great Exuberance.

MAY BECOME A NUISANCE.

Tradesmen Under No Obligation
to Contribute to Success of
Social Functions.

That President Murphy of the Chica-
Cubs is not in sympathy with all the metho-
employed by the local organizations of roo-
ers to create enthusiasm in advance of the
coming pennant races was demonstrated yesterday by the receipt of advance copies of an
article written by him for an eastern magazine.

THE CHICAGO DAILY TRIBUNE:
MARCH 3, 1908.

ROOTERS TAKE UP THE GAGE

Sharp Retort by Cubs' Admirers
to Criticism of Murphy.

LETTER OF PROTEST SENT.

West Side Club Formed to Advance All
Interests in That Section.

March 10, 1908

ROOTERS MAY NOT BE ABLE TO KEEP QUIET.

LEFT OUT? NUTS!

The 1908 season had many firsts. As noted previously, the phrase "get your goat" is thought to have originated that year. The phase "way out in left field," meaning someone out of touch with reality or confused, also is believed to have originated in that era. And it perhaps involved the Cubs.

Beyond the left-field wall at the Cubs park was the Neuropsychiatric Hospital, a mental institution. The residents (or inmates, depending on the severity of their condition) were known to make strange noises and even stranger remarks. Fans and players could hear sounds made by the asylum's patients, who were "way out in left field."

CHICAGO MAY HAVE TO STOP ALL UNNECESSARY NOISES, INCLUDING THE POLITICAL
CAMPAIGN, FOR A COUPLE OF WEEKS.

STAY AWAY FROM THE WINDOWS

In October 1908, as the Cubs battled Detroit in the World Series, the *Daily News* made multiple mentions, backed up by the local coroner, that a loss could lead to physical and mental calamity among the local populace.

"IF CUBS LOSE, SUICIDE, ASSERTS CORONER"

"HOFFMAN MAKES GREWSOME PROPHECY"

"FANS LOSING THEIR REASON"

"If the Cubs don't win the pennant—tragedy, despair, insanity, suicide, coroner's inquest, and a new chapter in baseball history."

In New York, the situation was much the same. On October 13, the *Chicago Tribune* ran this article:

CHICAGO TRIBUNE OCTOBER 13, 1908

DEATHS DUE TO BALL CRAZE.

New York Health Department Blames Close Finish for Increase in Heart Failures.

New York, Oct. 12.—Deaths from heart disease increased last week, due, the health department physicians say, to the acute baseball situation.

Last week the deaths were 154, as compared with 129 for the corresponding week in 1907. In Manhattan the deaths were seventy, as compared with fifty-eight, showing, in the opinion of physicians, that the interest in the game had spread throughout the city.

For the week ended Oct. 3 before a final decision regarding the disputed game with Chi-

The "acute baseball situation" mentioned in the article was brought on by the Cubs, and by what came to be known in baseball lore as "Merkle's Boner."

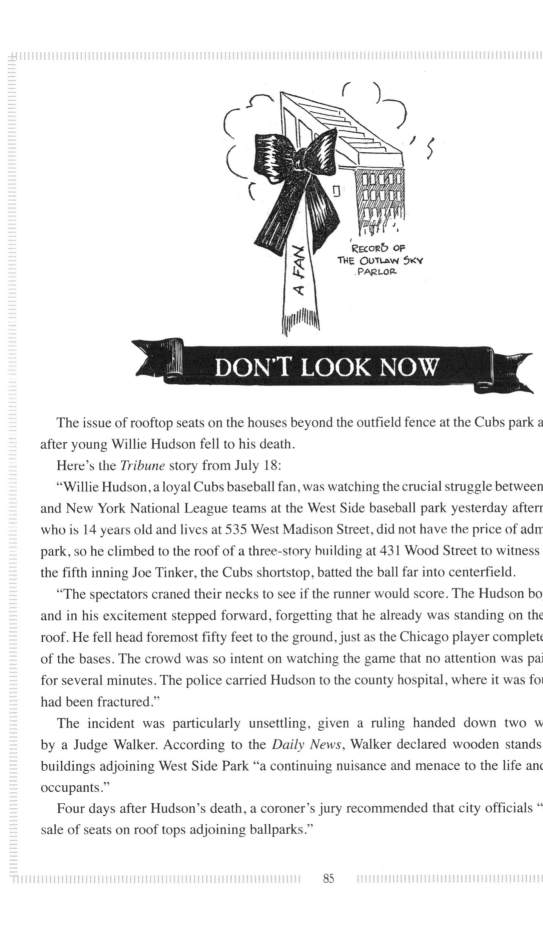

RECORD OF
THE OUTLAW SKY
PARLOR

A FAN

DON'T LOOK NOW

The issue of rooftop seats on the houses beyond the outfield fence at the Cubs park arose in 1908 after young Willie Hudson fell to his death.

Here's the *Tribune* story from July 18:

"Willie Hudson, a loyal Cubs baseball fan, was watching the crucial struggle between the Chicago and New York National League teams at the West Side baseball park yesterday afternoon. Willie, who is 14 years old and lives at 535 West Madison Street, did not have the price of admission to the park, so he climbed to the roof of a three-story building at 431 Wood Street to witness the game. In the fifth inning Joe Tinker, the Cubs shortstop, batted the ball far into centerfield.

"The spectators craned their necks to see if the runner would score. The Hudson boy jumped up and in his excitement stepped forward, forgetting that he already was standing on the edge of the roof. He fell head foremost fifty feet to the ground, just as the Chicago player completed the circuit of the bases. The crowd was so intent on watching the game that no attention was paid to the boy for several minutes. The police carried Hudson to the county hospital, where it was found his skull had been fractured."

The incident was particularly unsettling, given a ruling handed down two weeks earlier by a Judge Walker. According to the *Daily News*, Walker declared wooden stands on roofs of buildings adjoining West Side Park "a continuing nuisance and menace to the life and limb of the occupants."

Four days after Hudson's death, a coroner's jury recommended that city officials "suppress the sale of seats on roof tops adjoining ballparks."

THE CHICAGO DAILY TRIBUNE:

May 2, 1908

MODERN MILLINERY VS. THE BASEBALL FAN.

BROAD VIEW OF FASHION

A "Merry Widow" irritated just about every man who came in contact with one.

The Merry Widow was a 1905 operetta that enjoyed great success in Europe before arriving in the United States. The production included elaborate costumes that inspired female fashion of the day. One of the most popular pieces was an oversized hat that women seemingly wore everywhere, including the ballpark. Spectators seated behind a female wearing a "Merry Widow" were annoyed, at the least.

Cubs catcher Johnny Kling measured the size of his wife's hat—it was three and one-half feet, end to end—and figured that if he put one behind him during games he never again would be charged with a passed ball.

"While the hat would make a dandy auxiliary backstop for me, I'm glad my wife wouldn't let me have it," Kling said. "The problem of transportation is too severe. Did you notice us on the night ride [during spring training] from Chattanooga to Birmingham? Say, that was fierce. My wife curled up in one seat of the double section and slept. I sat on the armrest of the other seat and played night watchman for her hat. It filled the seat and hung over the edge.

"There was no place to hang the hat or a paper bag big enough to put it in, and I was too tired to roll the thing up and down the car aisle. She wouldn't let me stand it up on the rear platform of the coach, so I just sat there and watched it."

Women took the fashion statement seriously.

"A large feminine fan with a merry widow lid of pronounced blue tint, two stories high, and adorned with sweeping feathers, insisted on standing directly in front of some of the box seats on the third base side of the catcher," the *Tribune* reported after an Cubs game in August. "She was deaf to all remarks and requests to remove the beautiful creation, but when a policeman politely asked her to take it off or sit down she and her escort left in a terrible huff, looking for Prex Murphy [Cubs president Charles W. Murphy] or anybody else to pay damages for her fatally injured feelings."

ABOLISHING THE BIG-HAT NUISANCE IN BALL PARKS.

EVEN IN HIS DREAMS HE HEARS TH

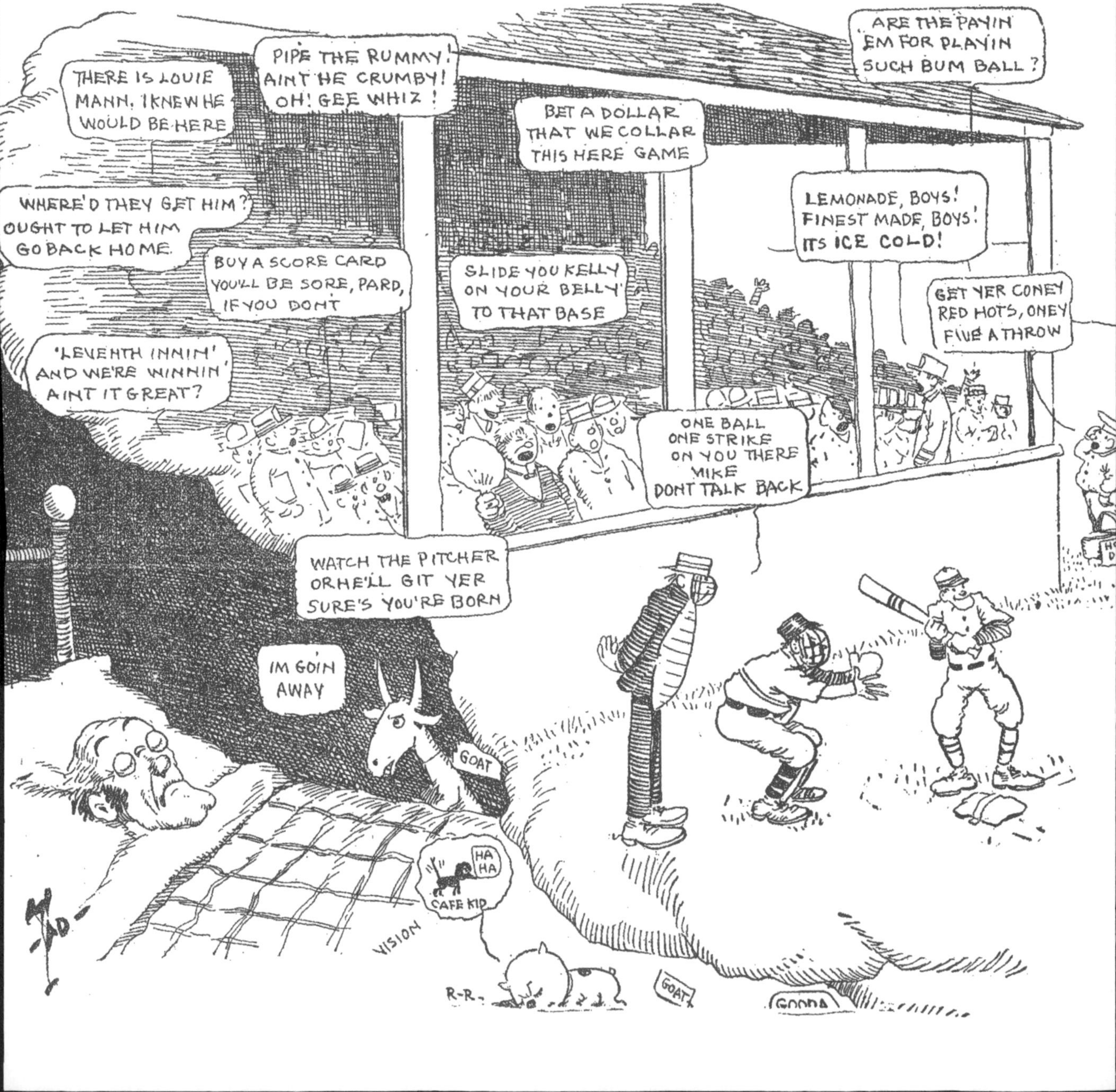

"MERRY WIDOW" WALTZ.---BY TAD.

THE FAMOUS 'MERRY WIDOW' WALTZ

New Words for Season's Musical Hit, Written by Beatrice Fairfax

BY BEATRICE FAIRFAX.

Was there ever such a bewitching, haunting, swaying melody as the "Merry Widow" Waltz? It only needed words to make it perfect, and here they are.

Cut out the music and paste it on a cardboard and without cost you will be the possessor of a piece of music that would otherwise have cost you twenty-five cents, and that would be merely the music, not the words.

It is music that will sing itself into the heads of both young and old. Try it on the piano in your home.

To the boys and girls of yesterday it brings memories of dim drawing rooms on Summer evenings when some one played softly on the piano and two happy young things waltzed dreamily and silently together and dreamed that they had found the road to paradise.

To the boys and girls of to-day the pictures are all of the future.

SONG BY BEATRICE FAIRFAX FOR THE "MERRY WIDOW" WALTZ

I.
SOFTLY calling,
The enthralling
Music chants.
Come and glide, dear,
Lightly glide, dear,
Through the dance.
When I hold you close, dear,
Skies seem ever blue.
All the world seems made for love
And just us two.

In Love's Paradise we will live,
While the perfume of Spring fills the air.
We are borne along on the wings of a song
(Musical interlude)
Let sadness take flight for the day,
There is naught in the world that may harm.
With young hearts of May we will dance care away,
And laugh at grim Winter's alarm.

II.
WE'LL go swinging,
Gayly winging,
On our way;
Lights are flashing,
And the plashing
Fountains play.
Through the room we'll whirl, dear,
Happy moments through;
Gladly, gladly will I come
And waltz with you.

What is life without music and song?
What is love if there's sorrow as well?
There is joy on the wing—catch it all who
can sing.
(Musical interlude)
May the rose's blush color our dreams,
As our hearts with the melody thrill,
And we'll dance by bright streams, where
the merry sunbeams
Splash gold o'er each rippling rill.

III.
LEAVE all sorrow
For to-morrow,
What care we?
Care and troubles
Are but bubbles,
Let them flee.
While the music calls us,
Heaven smiles above;
I forgot all else, my own,
But you and love.

With hearts ever young, let us dance
As long as the music holds sway.
Your hand, dear, in mine, and my soul's love
thine.
(Musical interlude)
And memory shall cherish the joy,
To give forth again in the years,
When our dancing is o'er and we draw on
her store
Of the sweet past that banishes tears.

THE MERRY WIDOW WALTZ-SONG
From Melodies by FRANZ LEHAR Copyright, 1908, by the New York Evening Journal Publishing Co. Arr. by THEODORE MORSE

THE HATS WERE BAD...

BUT THE SONG WAS WORSE

As much as Cubs fans disliked the large Merry Widow hats, nothing compared with their distaste for the "Merry Widow Waltz."

The song seemed almost omnipresent during the 1908 season. With brass bands at most games, the song was played relentlessly as a way of distracting the opposing team. Boston's Royal Rooters used the same tactics with a song of their own, "Tessie."

Unfortunately for Cubs fans, the opposing team eventually left town, but the "Merry Widow Waltz" played on and on.

"ALL RIGHT ... LET ME HEAR YA. ... AH ONE ... AH TWO ... AH THREE ..."

—HARRY CARAY

"Take Me Out to the Ball Game" made its debut in 1908, thanks to Jack Norworth (lyrics) and Albert Von Tilzer (music). Experts concluded that it probably took the pair less than an hour to come up with what turned into an immediate hit and an instant classic. The version by Billy Murray and Haydn Quartet hit the top of the charts on October 31, 1908, and stayed there for seven weeks.

In 2008, "Take Me Out to the Ball Game" was the third most-performed song in America, trailing only "Happy Birthday" and "The Star-Spangled Banner."

When Harry Caray joined the Cubs as a broadcaster in 1982, he brought along the practice of leading the crowd in the seventh-inning singing of "Take Me Out to the Ball Game." The tradition started during Harry's years with the White Sox, where owner Bill Veeck first coaxed a reluctant Harry into showing off his singing skill.

A famous song made even more famous by Harry with ties back to 1908? Coincidence? For DePorter, it was just another circumstantial curiosity.

HIGGINS
©1987 CHICAGO SUN-TIMES

LIGHT YEARS AHEAD

The debate over lights at Cubs home games raged for many years. One could say the roots of the debate were sown in 1908. The idea was born of the fact that more fans could attend games because doubleheaders could feature both day and night games with tickets sold for each.

Cincinnati Reds president Garry Herrmann and inventor George P. Cahill of Holyoke, Massachusetts, devised a plan in 1908 that would allow for fans to watch baseball at night. The Reds planned to erect five one-hundred-foot steel towers with twin searchlights on each tower.

"The lights will be so arranged that they will not shine into the eyes of the fielders except where an infielder is compelled to run directly facing the outfield after a ball, and then he will not be handicapped as much as a man who usually plays a sun field," Herrmann told the *Sporting Life* magazine in August. "I have investigated the scheme thoroughly and I am convinced that it will be a big success. We expect to have the plant installed in time for the Reds return from their next Eastern trip and hope to give a series of games under the new system before the season closes. If the innovation works as well as we expect it to, baseball will be revolutionized, for it will be possible for us then to cater to a large mass of people during the week who heretofore have had their opportunities for seeing games restricted to Sunday exhibitions."

What does this have to do with the Cubs? Given the strange incidence of the number eight throughout DePorter's research, he was reminded of the Cubs' first scheduled night game at Wrigley Field: 08.08.88. The game was rained out and played the following night, but the point is well taken.

In 1908, Herrmann had light towers installed in Cincinnati. On September 29, the lights shined—figuratively at least—on Joe Tinker and the Cubs.

In an afternoon game, after a walk to Artie Hofman in the second inning, Tinker hit a ball that bounced over Dode Paskert's head and disappeared into the enclosure at the base of the tower in center field. While the outfielder tried in vain to retrieve the ball, Tinker circled the bases for a home run. There were no ground rules to cover such a circumstance. The Cubs won, 5-2, and moved past the New York Giants into first place.

The Reds were the first major league team to play host to a night game, but it didn't happen until 1935.

BASEBALL IN THE NIGHT TIME.

AN ANATOMICAL ERROR

BRIGGS '08

THE CHICAGO DAILY TRIBUNE:
SATURDAY. MARCH 14, 1908.

JOINT HOODOO NO
TERROR TO CUBS.

Train No. 13, with 13 Cars,
Reaches Vicksburg on Time
on Friday, March 13.

THE FURTHER DEPORTER DUG, THE DEEPER THE HOODOO.

"I don't think it's unreasonable to say that a majority of Cubs fans—me included—believe at some level that something, a hoodoo, is responsible for all that has happened or failed to happen since 1908," DePorter said.

"The depth of people's beliefs in hoodoos in 1908 made it clear to me that I was searching the right time in history. It's incredible the degree to which fans, writers, cartoonists, and ordinary citizens took seriously the notion of hoodoos."

One of DePorter's greatest hoodoo discoveries came not from researching 1908, but from a conversation in 2008 with Ernie Banks. Mr. Cub told of his own brush with the supernatural. Ernie talked about a particular form of hoodoo called voodoo. When he was fifteen, a local practitioner told his mother Essie that he would one day be famous and well known. Two years later, Ernie's mother directed her husband Eddie to take Ernie to a woman in Palestine, Texas, who practiced voodoo. The woman predicted a future in baseball for Ernie. The rest, as they say, is history.

Puzzle: Who Threw the Cracker?

Banks remembered the infamous black cat that scampered across the Shea Stadium field when the Cubs and the New York Mets, battling for the National League pennant, were playing in September 1969. It was hoodoo to be sure, and by all accounts the Mets knew exactly what they had unleashed.

What better way to connect the dots, as it were, between 1908 and perhaps the most infamous Cubs failure of all than to hear the inside, never-before-published account from Mr. Cub himself.

VOODOO, HOODOO

AND THE REAL STORY OF A BLACK CAT

In Louisiana, hoodoo is better known as voodoo, a powerful combination of culture, religion, and superstition.

As a young man growing up in Dallas, Ernie Banks knew enough about the mystery and magic to have a healthy respect for the underlying power. To locals, including Ernie's mother Essie, it was one of many religious flavors that traced its roots to West Africa. Essie brought the traditions and practices into her marriage with Eddie Banks and passed them on to her children.

"My mother was born in Louisiana," Ernie said. "They call it Louisiana voodoo. It's something she believed in and something we were raised with. It is all about magical things, tinctures, healing with dance, and music mixed in. It's a whole lot of things I don't understand."

"They read your spirit," Ernie said. "My mother talked my dad into taking me to a woman in Palestine, Texas, when I was about seventeen years old."

"I WAS JUST LISTENING AND WATCHING. SHE LIT A CANDLE AND STARTED TALKING TO MY FATHER ABOUT WHAT I WOULD DO IN LIFE. SHE READ MY SPIRIT AND SAID THAT I WOULDN'T GO INTO THE ARMY, BUT I WOULD PLAY BASEBALL."

More than twenty years later, on a September night in Shea Stadium, the memory of his experience in Palestine, Texas, rose up inside of Mr. Cub. Though they couldn't have known how hopeless their battle was at the time, the Cubs got a glimpse of the future on September 9, 1969, when a black cat ran across the infield. A highly superstitious team led by a deeply superstitious manager, the Cubs were shaken.

HOO-RAY THE CUBS HAVE SETTLED DOWN AND HAVE LEASED THEIR SWELL APARTMENT FOR ANOTHER YEAR

"Leo Durocher, our manager, was very superstitious,"
Banks said. "He didn't like black cats crossing in front of him.
He didn't like going up the stairs and passing somebody.
He'd wear the same uniform when we were winning. He had a lot
of those little things. I think a lot of athletes have those traits,
or superstitions. Leo had them; a lot of managers did. I didn't
understand it until I looked back on my life and remembered my
dad taking me to see the lady who practiced voodooism."

The black cat, appearing seemingly out of nowhere, scampered onto the field, past Cubs third baseman Ron Santo, and paused in the on-deck circle on the third-base side. The feline surveyed the Cubs dugout, then scurried away. The Cubs had arrived in New York clinging to a two-game lead in the standings, an advantage that had shrunk from a nine-game lead on August 16. The two-game series would prove to be their undoing–the Cubs lost both games and never regained first place.

On his way to the clubhouse after the second game, Banks saw a Mets clubhouse attendant whom he had befriended over his career.

"Did you guys bring in that cat?" Banks asked. "WAS THAT A METS CAT?"

The attendant shrugged and turned his palms and head toward the sky. With a mischievous twinkle in his eyes, he flashed a sheepish smile.

Not a word was needed to confirm the hoodoo. The Mets had let the cat out of the bag, in more ways than one.

Banks could only shake his head. He knew something about the extraordinary, and the black-cat affair reminded him of his trip to Palestine, Texas.

CHICAGO DAILY NEWS

FRIDAY, FEBRUARY 14, 1908.

BASEBALL FANS HAVE HAD AN UNEASY REST.

THERE ARE LIMITS EVEN IN THE
FORTUNE TELLING BUSINESS

Located about one hundred miles southeast of Dallas, Palestine was a thriving town, thanks to the oil industry. Ernie and his father reached their destination, stretched their legs, and knocked on the door of the voodoo priestess.

She looked Ernie up and down, closed her eyes, and took a deep breath. Then another. And another. She opened her eyes and turned her attention away from the youngster, focusing instead on Ernie's father.

"Is he gonna go into the Army?" the elder Banks wondered.

"No," the woman replied firmly. "He's going to play baseball."

"That's what my father wanted to know: whether or not I was going to be a baseball player," Ernie said. "My mother wanted to know whether or not I was going into the Army."

Eddie Banks was both a pitcher and catcher for the Dallas Green Monarchs and Black Giants in the Negro Leagues. His first son, Ernie, the second of twelve children in the family, was going to play baseball. Jackie Robinson had broken Major League Baseball's color barrier the previous year, 1947.

"My dad just smiled a little bit," Ernie said of hearing the woman's prediction. "He didn't talk very much. Then we drove back to Dallas, and that was it. From then on, he was out playing catch with me every day after he got off work."

Eddie and Essie came from substantially different religious backgrounds. Ernie's paternal great-grandfather was a minister. Still, Eddie respected voodoo.

"I DID GO INTO THE ARMY, BUT I HURT MY KNEE AND WENT OVER TO GERMANY, WHERE I PLAYED BASEBALL," ERNIE SAID. "I NEVER WENT TO BASIC TRAINING BECAUSE OF THE KNEE INJURY. SO HER PROJECTION, AS I LOOK BACK ON IT, PRETTY MUCH CAME TRUE."

"My outfit went to Germany. A friend of mine, Ronald Gilmore, knew that I played baseball. It was April, and they were choosing a baseball team for the company. He put my name on the list. I did pretty well playing in the Army. The scouts saw me play and they remembered me. When I came back, the [Negro League Kansas City] Monarchs signed me up."

From there, Banks joined the Cubs and became the team's first African-American player. Years later, of no surprise to Essie Banks, Ernie was as well known as any player in baseball.

"One of the voodoo people told my mother that I would be a very famous person one day," he said. "They told her that about me when I was around fifteen. They had this feeling about me."

It's the same feeling Cubs fans have had about Ernie since the day Mr. Cub arrived in Chicago.

Baseball players have always been superstitious, and the 1908 Cubs hardly were an exception. Their list of superstitions is as long as it is humorous.

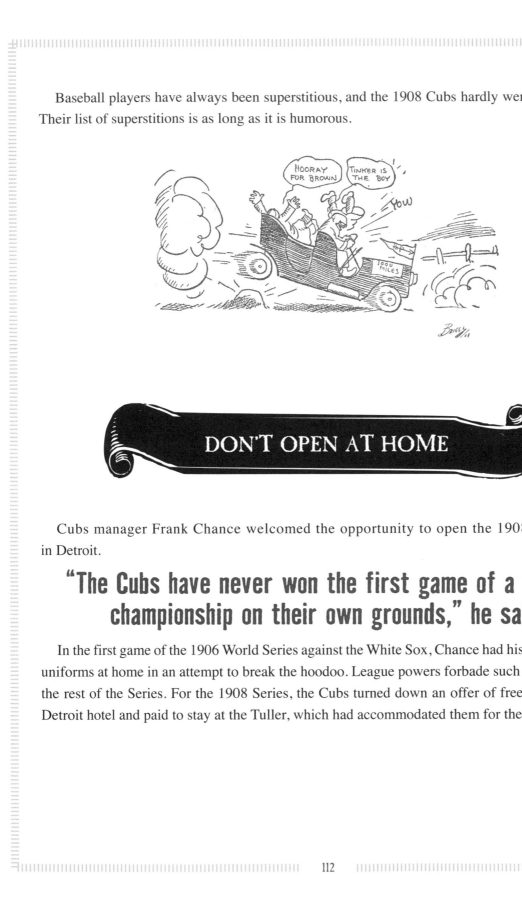

DON'T OPEN AT HOME

Cubs manager Frank Chance welcomed the opportunity to open the 1908 World Series in Detroit.

"The Cubs have never won the first game of a world's championship on their own grounds," he said.

In the first game of the 1906 World Series against the White Sox, Chance had his team wear road uniforms at home in an attempt to break the hoodoo. League powers forbade such shenanigans for the rest of the Series. For the 1908 Series, the Cubs turned down an offer of free lodging from a Detroit hotel and paid to stay at the Tuller, which had accommodated them for the 1907 Series.

PUPPY VS. HOODOO: PUPPY WINS

Superstitions trumped everything, including rank. When the 1908 Cubs suffered through a bad stretch on the road, team owner Charles W. Murphy returned home early because he feared he was responsible for the poor showing.

A Boston bull pup took Murphy's spot on the Cubs bench.

"President Murphy left for Chicago early in the afternoon," reported the *Tribune*. "It was his belief he was the hoodoo, and no one questions his word in face of the result. [Outfielder] Frank Schulte's Boston bull pup 'Cub,' which was given him by [backup catcher] Pat Moran, was sent from Boston and sat on the Cubs' bench. Pat swears the pup was responsible for the reversal of form. 'Cub' is to [be] taken to Chicago with the team."

Mascots were potential hoodoo-busters, along with just about anything else an afflicted team could dream up. For instance, on August 21, 1908, the *Chicago Daily News* reported: "Yesterday the Cubs came out in brand-new black hosiery, with no rings or marks of any kind. They worked well for a start so far as ball players' superstition goes. The black sox will remain in high favor if the team makes a spurt and climbs to the top."

UNFURLING THE MYSTERY OF HISTORY

"When luck began to break against the Cubs just as they were starting east President Murphy declared he would burn that yellow pennant, for he believed it a hoodoo for the world's champions. The flag is gone, the red-trimmed blue banner of the league is in its place."

Chicago Daily News, June 25, 1908

Among the Cubs' first activities of the 1908 season was to raise flags over West Side Grounds for winning the National League pennant and the World Series the previous season. The events didn't go off smoothly, which likely rattled many hoodoo detectives.

Here's the *Daily News'* account of the April 22 struggles to raise the National League pennant

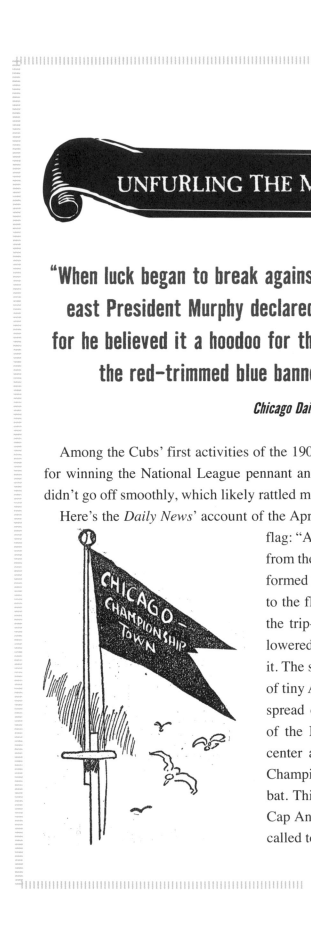

flag: "A band led, followed by the champions. They marched from the Cubs' bench to the coop of the visitors and the Reds formed in line behind them, then all marched across left field to the flagpole in deep center. The pennant was hoisted but the trip-string failed to slip the first time and the flag was lowered until [groundskeeper] Charlie Kuhn could readjust it. The second time it went up the pennant unfurled, a bunch of tiny American flags fluttered to the ground and the breeze spread out the bunting, disclosing to the fans the emblem of the National league championship—a blue flag, in the center a white baseball with the words 'National League Champions—1907,' and a huge white cub, holding a baseball bat. This ceremony over, the teams turned to the game and Cap Anson [the legendary Cubs star of a previous era] was called to the center of the diamond to pitch the first ball."

The Cubs won that day. However, after the world championship banner-raising ceremony on May 21, they lost to the Boston Doves, 11-3. "Unfurling a world's flag is a hoodoo champions do not appear able to overcome," the *Daily News* reported the following day. "New York tried it against Cincinnati [in 1906] and failed; the Chicago White Stockings broke their pennant pole when theirs was hoisted [in 1907] and then a big storm prevented the game; yesterday the Cubs got their trimming right in line with the usual performance."

BLACK CAT: BLACK MAGIC.

It's one thing to see a black cat, perhaps the most notorious carrier of bad luck. It's quite another when your city hosts a black cat convention, particularly in a year that birthed the greatest hoodoo of all time. It happened in Chicago in 1908.

On September 11, the *Tribune* reported on the Concatenated Order of Hoo Hoos, the black-cat group that gathered at the Auditorium Hotel.

"Forty initiates were introduced to the mysteries and secrets of the Concatenated Order of Hoo Hoos on the ninth floor of the Auditorium hotel last night. The session was known as a session-on-the-fence, the hoo hoos representing black cats on a fence after dark. John S. Bonner, snark of the universe, presided at the ceremonies."

Just as any goat-related hoodoo originated in 1908, the same can be said of the black-cat hoodoo, which preyed on the Cubs in a September 1969 game at Shea Stadium in New York.

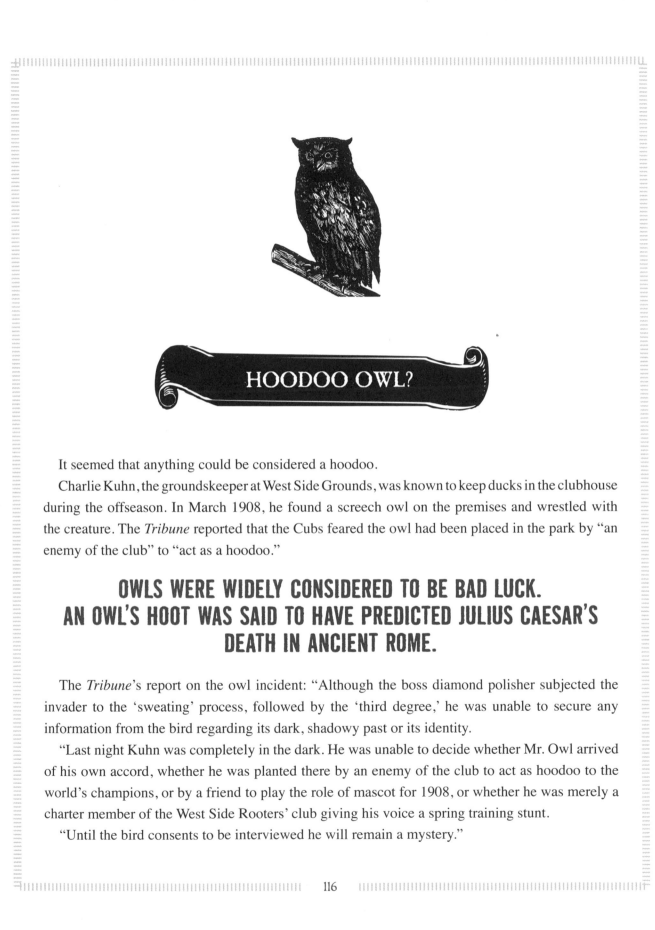

HOODOO OWL?

It seemed that anything could be considered a hoodoo.

Charlie Kuhn, the groundskeeper at West Side Grounds, was known to keep ducks in the clubhouse during the offseason. In March 1908, he found a screech owl on the premises and wrestled with the creature. The *Tribune* reported that the Cubs feared the owl had been placed in the park by "an enemy of the club" to "act as a hoodoo."

OWLS WERE WIDELY CONSIDERED TO BE BAD LUCK. AN OWL'S HOOT WAS SAID TO HAVE PREDICTED JULIUS CAESAR'S DEATH IN ANCIENT ROME.

The *Tribune*'s report on the owl incident: "Although the boss diamond polisher subjected the invader to the 'sweating' process, followed by the 'third degree,' he was unable to secure any information from the bird regarding its dark, shadowy past or its identity.

"Last night Kuhn was completely in the dark. He was unable to decide whether Mr. Owl arrived of his own accord, whether he was planted there by an enemy of the club to act as hoodoo to the world's champions, or by a friend to play the role of mascot for 1908, or whether he was merely a charter member of the West Side Rooters' club giving his voice a spring training stunt.

"Until the bird consents to be interviewed he will remain a mystery."

HEN-PECKED

White Sox owner Charles Comiskey knew his team needed all the help it could get for the 1906 World Series against the Cubs. His "Hitless Wonders," as the White Sox had been dubbed, seemingly were no match for a Cubs team that went 116-38, the most dominating regular season performance in baseball history.

Comiskey, at "great financial cost," according to the media, went to the west side of the city, where the Cubs played, bought what came to be known as the Hoodoo Hen, and placed her on the field. Though the mascot got off to a slow start, she proved to be worth every penny that Comiskey paid for her, as the White Sox caught fire and won the American League pennant.

The Hoodoo Hen, however, apparently didn't enjoy all the attention, according to an October 12 report in the *Tribune*: "Coming back to the Hoodoo Hen, she played her little part in center field, same as on the west side. Any one who knows the hen could see she didn't like the situation. They had rigged white stockings on her legs and tied a white ribbon about her swan-like neck. When not absorbed in the game the mascot gnawed at the white socks with her teeth. At other times, being a modest hen, she squatted in the grass. She knew that too much lingerie showed beneath her skirts, and the thought provoked her. If she is the same hen that made her debut in the previous game she is a mutt."

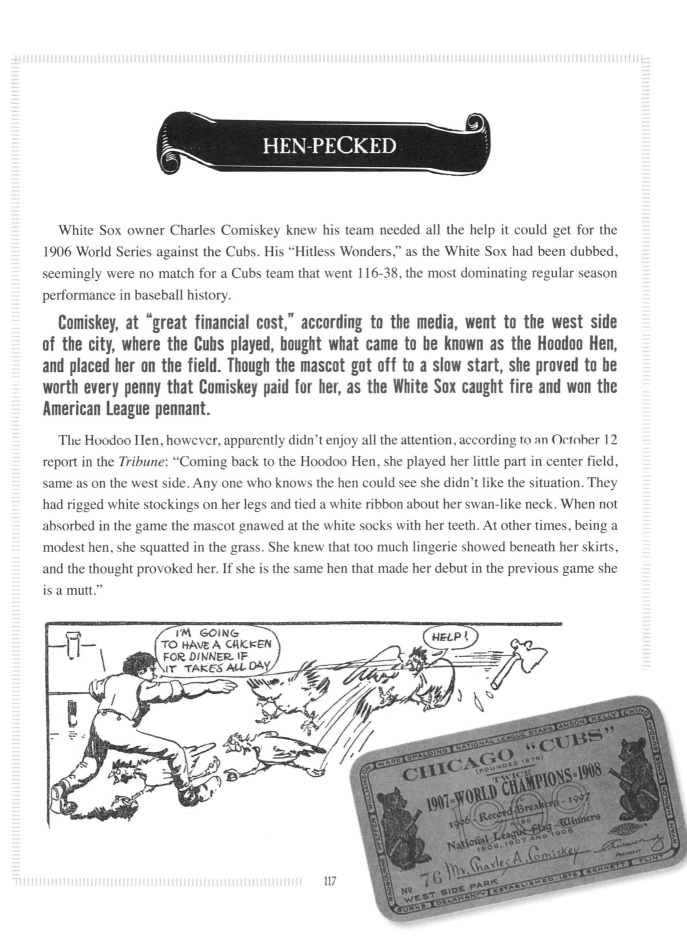

THAT FOOL KID WILL RISK ANYTHING

— AND THIS ONE JUST GOES ON HIS RECKLESS WAY
REGARDLESS

THERE'S NO ROMANCE IN BASEBALL

When word of Artie Hofman's engagement reached the newspapers—slightly to his dismay one February day in 1908—manager Frank Chance took note.

Hofman, a utility infielder/outfielder, had used his engagement as leverage in contract negotiations, although he had said he was content with the Cubs' offer. He claimed to have an offer outside of baseball that would have paid him $7,000 a year, more than his salary with the Cubs. Plus, his fiancé's family preferred someone in a more conventional line of work than baseball.

That summer, Hofman and his wife-to-be set a wedding date of September 7, a scheduled off-day for the Cubs. It was assumed the Cubs by that time would have a commanding lead over New York and Pittsburgh.

The weeks rolled by, and wedding plans were set. Invitations were ready to be sent. A preacher was selected to perform the ceremony. Everything was in order.

Well, almost everything. Chance informed Hofman there would be no wedding for any Cubs player in September. "When the season is over," Chance told Hofman. "For the good of the team."

Hofman was a good sport about it. "I guess Miss Looker and I can wait," he said. "She's as anxious to have the Cubs win as I am."

CHICAGO TRIBUNE   FEBRUARY 11, 1908

SCHULTE WAS NO PINHEAD

It wasn't that Cubs outfielder Frank Schulte didn't think extra batting practice would help. He just wanted to feather the effort by staying true to what he perceived to be a peculiar power of the hairpin. Schulte would search the ground for hairpins on his way to the ballpark. Here's a *Tribune* report from April 1908:

"Frank Schulte's odd little hairpin hunch, a superstition to increase his batting, has broken out again with renewed virulence this spring. Hairpins found by the wayside bring the horse owner luck at bat, he thinks, and bugs daily tote the hunches to the park and hand them over to Frank. There is no magic in a purchased pin. They must have been found in order to produce the goods. Here is the formula doped out by the hair-harpoon expert:

"An ordinary straight pin means a single to center. Should one of the prongs be bent outward that pin is good for a hit to right or left, as the case may be. The next larger sized pin signifies the two bagger; still larger, the three bagger; and the tortoise shell skewer for piercing the Psyche knot has been known to elicit a home run. Those tiny little inch and a half things they wear in the frizzled fronts mean safe bunts; but look out if the frizzle pin is bent upward, for that angle in the hunch indicates a fly bunt to the pitcher and the doubling up of the man at first base.

"Mr. Schulte is a decided favorite at the west side. While naturally a good hitter, he cannot thump so well without hairpins. Therefore, the thousands of fans who have the welfare of the Cubs at heart should keep their eyes peeled for hairpins and hand them over to Mr. Schulte just before each and every game. If the boys do their duty Frank should bat 1.200."

The *Daily News* recounted the inspired efforts of a female fan who sent "a long, straight one that looked good for a home run at least" to Schulte. Signing herself as E.E.R., the woman included a poem:

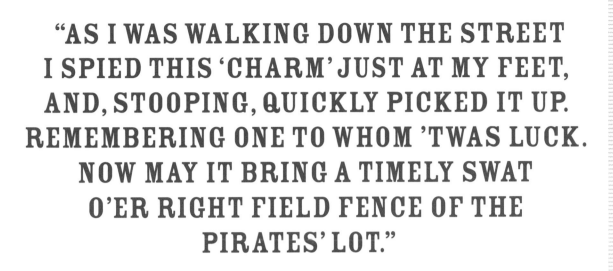

"AS I WAS WALKING DOWN THE STREET
I SPIED THIS 'CHARM' JUST AT MY FEET,
AND, STOOPING, QUICKLY PICKED IT UP.
REMEMBERING ONE TO WHOM 'TWAS LUCK.
NOW MAY IT BRING A TIMELY SWAT
O'ER RIGHT FIELD FENCE OF THE
PIRATES' LOT."

The Cubs hardly were alone when it came to superstitions. One major league pitcher believed a shutout was a hoodoo. If he entered the ninth inning without having allowed a run, he begged teammates to purposely drop fly balls or misplay grounders to ensure the other team would score at least one run.

OTHER CUBS SUPERSTITIONS

Manager/first baseman France Chance looked for four-leaf clovers before games.

Pitcher Ed Reulbach thought if he struck out the first batter, he would lose. It was a common superstition of the time.

Shortstop Joe Tinker walked in a straight line to home plate; if he made an out, he changed his route the next time.

Chance wanted to be in car number 13 on a train. He traveled on Friday the thirteenth in a thirteen-car train, in berth number 13 in his car. He believed a telephone call to his wife after he arrived at his destination would overcome the hoodoo.

Chance did not allow the team be photographed before the 1908 World Series.

Common superstitions of the era included:

NEVER TOUCH THE CATCHER'S MITT BEFORE A GAME.

NEVER PASS A FUNERAL PROCESSION ON THE WAY TO A GAME;
IF IT OCCURRED, TOSS A COIN TO REVERSE THE HOODOO.

A TEAM THAT PASSED A WAGON FULL OF UNBALED HAY ON THE WAY TO
A GAME WAS CONFIDENT IT WOULD WIN. A WAGON FULL OF EMPTY BARRELS WAS
ANOTHER SURE SIGN OF WINNING.

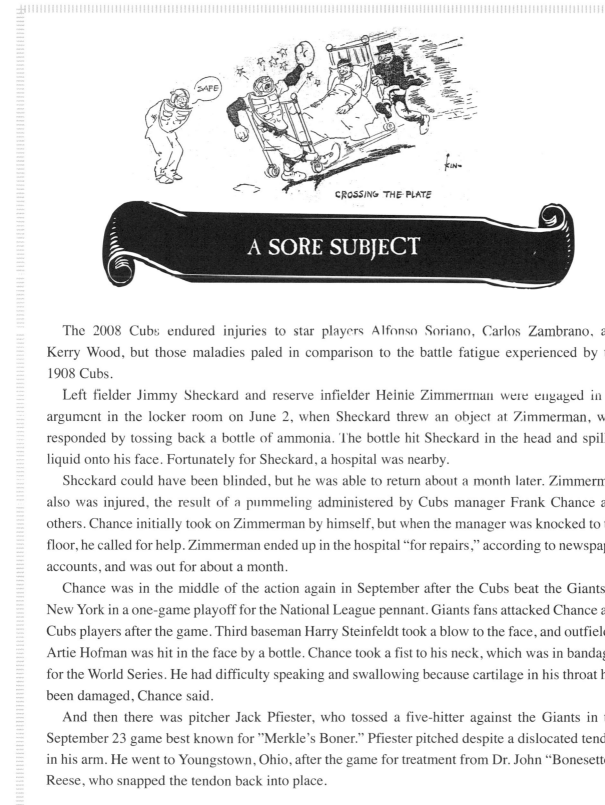

CROSSING THE PLATE

A SORE SUBJECT

The 2008 Cubs endured injuries to star players Alfonso Soriano, Carlos Zambrano, and Kerry Wood, but those maladies paled in comparison to the battle fatigue experienced by the 1908 Cubs.

Left fielder Jimmy Sheckard and reserve infielder Heinie Zimmerman were engaged in an argument in the locker room on June 2, when Sheckard threw an object at Zimmerman, who responded by tossing back a bottle of ammonia. The bottle hit Sheckard in the head and spilled liquid onto his face. Fortunately for Sheckard, a hospital was nearby.

Sheckard could have been blinded, but he was able to return about a month later. Zimmerman also was injured, the result of a pummeling administered by Cubs manager Frank Chance and others. Chance initially took on Zimmerman by himself, but when the manager was knocked to the floor, he called for help. Zimmerman ended up in the hospital "for repairs," according to newspaper accounts, and was out for about a month.

Chance was in the middle of the action again in September after the Cubs beat the Giants in New York in a one-game playoff for the National League pennant. Giants fans attacked Chance and Cubs players after the game. Third baseman Harry Steinfeldt took a blow to the face, and outfielder Artie Hofman was hit in the face by a bottle. Chance took a fist to his neck, which was in bandages for the World Series. He had difficulty speaking and swallowing because cartilage in his throat had been damaged, Chance said.

And then there was pitcher Jack Pfiester, who tossed a five-hitter against the Giants in the September 23 game best known for "Merkle's Boner." Pfiester pitched despite a dislocated tendon in his arm. He went to Youngstown, Ohio, after the game for treatment from Dr. John "Bonesetter" Reese, who snapped the tendon back into place.

SUGGESTIONS FOR CUBS

ADDITIONAL 1908 INJURIES TO CUBS PLAYERS:

• Chance: **MORTON'S DISEASE,** an inflamed and swollen nerve in the ball of one of his feet, bothered him after the 1907 season, and threatened to sideline him in 1908. Chance managed to avoid surgery.

• Shortstop Joe Tinker: Suffered **A GASH** on his left hand as the result of boxing with a hotel chandelier during spring training in Vicksburg, Mississippi. (That was Tinker's story.) Another report said he suffered the cut in an altercation with a parrot.

• Pfiester: His **THUMB BECAME STUCK IN A BOWLING BALL.** Not a permanent condition, although the ball did drag him halfway down a lane. The result was more embarrassment than physical torment.

• Hofman: **GASHED HAND,** the result of punching a lamp after reading a newspaper report suggesting the Cubs were lucky to have won a game. He needed stitches to close the wound.

• Pitcher Orval Overall: **STRAINED BACK,** suffered on Decoration Day (May 31) when he contorted his body trying to knock down a line drive. "It is believed a kidney has been torn loose," the *Sporting Life* reported. Apparently the publication was loose with facts—Overall returned to play a key part in the Cubs' success.

• Outfielder Frank Schulte:
APPENDICITIS.

• Outfielder Del Howard:
BROKEN HAND.

• Second baseman Johnny Evers:
STRAINED HIP and
BROKEN INDEX FINGER.
Neither injury kept him out of the lineup.

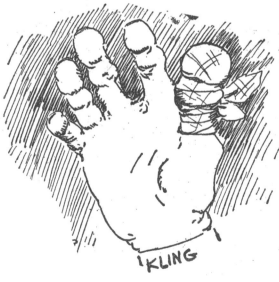

Merkle.
One name says it all.
Boner.
One word explains why.

On the morning of September 23, 1908, Fred Merkle woke up as a nineteen-year-old first baseman struggling to secure longterm employment with the New York Giants. Twenty-four hours later he was known throughout the baseball world for all the wrong reasons.

Unless, of course, you were a Cubs fan. In that case, "Merkle's Boner" was reason to cheer.

Merkle was on first base and Moose McCormick was on third with two outs in the bottom of the ninth in a 1-1 game at the Polo Grounds. When Al Bridwell singled to center, McCormick crossed the plate, and the Giants appeared to have won a critical game in a tight pennant race.

But in the chaos that followed, Cubs second baseman Johnny Evers never took his eyes off Merkle, who had stopped running to second and instead headed for the clubhouse in center field.

As Giants fans flooded the field, Evers told outfielder Artie Hofman to throw the ball to him. Hofman's throw sailed toward third base, where Giants pitcher Joe McGinnity had been doubling as third-base coach. Cubs shortstop Joe Tinker wrestled McGinnity for the ball. McGinnity, with Tinker pinned to the ground on his back, tossed the ball into the crowd beyond third base. Seldom-used Cubs pitcher Rube Kroh then made the play of his career. Spying the fan with the ball, Kroh asked for it. When the fan refused, Kroh slugged him and took the ball. Fighting the crowd, Kroh made his way to Evers, who was still near second base. Evers took the ball and stepped on the bag.

The Cubs appealed to umpire Hank O'Day, who had rejected a similar play in a 1-0 Cubs loss in Pittsburgh on September 4. O'Day ruled that Merkle was out on a force play, and since it was the third out, McCormick's run didn't count. Fearing for their lives (justifiably so), O'Day and fellow umpire Bob Emslie received police protection as they departed the ballpark. That night in his report to National League president Harry Pulliam, O'Day declared the game a tie.

Ironically, the "good of the league policy" came into play on behalf of the Cubs. Earlier in the season, the National League feared the Cubs' dominance was harmful to baseball. The "good of the league policy" dictated giving opposing teams every benefit of the doubt in games against the Cubs as a way of leveling the playing field. When O'Day ruled against the Cubs in the Pittsburgh game, the team protested with such an intensity, and so many threats were made, that O'Day had no choice but to follow the rulebook when the situation repeated itself in the Cubs-Giants game.

Merkle spent the rest of his life known for a mistake that tainted an otherwise long and successful baseball career. Well, mostly successful.

Merkle ended his career in 1920—with the Cubs. He played in five World Series and his team lost every one of them, including the 1918 Series with the Cubs. Bridwell also ended his career with the Cubs, in 1913.

As embarrassing as the incident was for Merkle, it didn't compare to the impact it had on Pulliam. Not only had the game been played in the media capital of the world, but Giants manager John McGraw's belligerence was legendary. With fans and team owners also no doubt outraged by the decision and exerting tremendous pressure, the troubled Pulliam committed suicide early in the 1909 season.

THE CHICAGO DAILY TRIBUNE: FRIDAY, OCTOBER 9, 1908.

AT A LATE HOUR LAST NIGHT MERKLE WAS SEEN CROSSING THE CANADA LINE.

POOR LITTLE OLD NEW YORK.

TWO FINISHES.

HOODOO? WHO CARES?

The more DePorter studied the 1908 season, the more he realized the hoodoo originated off the field. The Cubs simply endured too much to have been a party to a hoodoo of the magnitude that afflicted future Cubs teams.

The *Daily News* carried a stirring account of the Cubs' victory over the Giants in their one-game playoff for the National League pennant:

"Chicago's victory yesterday was one of the greatest on record. It was snatched from the rioting Giants, who thought they had it cinched and packed away when they scored in the first inning and the 'Peerless Mathewson' was on the slab; they won in spite of the obstacles put in their path by the board of directors when they compelled the Chicago club to make a hurried jump of nearly a thousand miles to meet the Giants on their home grounds; they won in spite of all the rowdy tactics of McGraw's gang of ball players, who did everything in their power to provoke a fight with the Chicago men before the game, and who slugged a number of them after it was over as they were threading their way thorough the mob of fanatics to the clubhouse.

"They won it in spite of the 'good of the league policy,' which was announced at the opening of the season, meaning the defeat of the Chicago club; they won in the greatest uphill fight in which any ball club was ever engaged, being called on to display the sterling qualities of gameness and nerve during adversity, and steady perseverance and faith in their superiority over all opponents; they won, even thought laboring for months under the severest handicap that can be imposed on a ball club, injuries that kept the team broken up for more than two months, spoiling its machine-like precision of both offense and defense.

"In a word, Frank Chance's Cubs have proven their title as the greatest aggregation ever gathered on a diamond, game, true and loyal to the core."

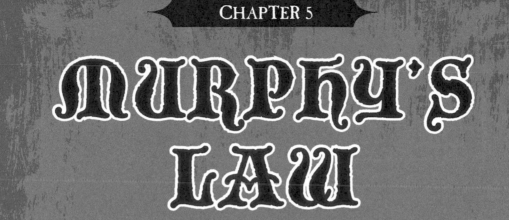

CHAPTER 5

MURPHY'S LAW

FOR DEPORTER,
THE PROCESS
HAD BEEN SIMILAR
TO THAT OF
THOMAS EDISON:
DISCOVERY BORN
OUT OF FAILURE

W

hen the moment came, it arrived as a whisper in a mind filled with facts, figures, and all manner of hoodoo. DePorter doesn't remember the hour or even the day—all he knows for sure is what triggered his intuition.

Months of research, and the absolute belief that the source of the Cubs' unprecedented World Series drought originated in 1908, had sharpened DePorter's senses. A postseason dinner that legendary entertainer George M. Cohan threw for the Cubs following their 1908 World Series victory triggered DePorter's intuition. What followed confirmed his suspicions. First, he had to find out which players attended the dinner, where it took place, and most importantly, who didn't attend.

For DePorter, the process had been similar to that of Thomas Edison: Discovery born out of failure. When lightning struck and the light bulb came on, it produced a sense of confirmation for DePorter rather than a burst of euphoria. Charles W. Murphy, the Cubs owner, had become a person of extreme interest. First, the facts:

The night after the Cubs won the 1908 World Series, Cohan hosted a celebratory dinner for the team at Rector's Restaurant in Chicago. As reported in the *Chicago Tribune* on Friday, October 16, 1908:

George Cohan gave a first performance last night the premier of the season of feasting and dining and wining and toasting and eulogizing the victorious Cubs. He pulled off the show "after his show" at Rector's and a pleasant time was had.

For fear that he might not be able to cope single handed with the Ursini Colossi Cohan brought along a team of theatrical pals, who played their positions with great skill.

Between innings "liquid and solid" happy remarks and lovely compliments were tossed and batted back and forth over the table. No errors.

Mons. Jean Finnegan poured and Sig. Banko Cregiere made the musical welken ring. Mr. Cohans,s guests were: Mr. and Mrs. Chance, Mr. and Mrs. Tinker, Mr. and Mrs. Steinfeldt, Mr. and Mrs. Howard, Mr. and Mrs. Sheckard, John J. Evers, Pat Moran, Charles Williams.

"Before reading about the dinner my instincts told me that whatever the nature of the Cubs' hoodoo, it had nothing to do with the players or the fans," DePorter said. "The team overcame extreme odds and hoodoos of every flavor to win the World Series. And the fans were there every step of way with passion and overwhelming support. What caught my eye was the fact that one person in particular had been excluded from the dinner, purposely. And that was Murphy."

Murphy was so universally disliked that the players actually voted on whether he should be invited to the dinner. The vote was unanimous:

NO MURPHY.

Murphy's list of transgressions against fans and players had mounted in 1908:

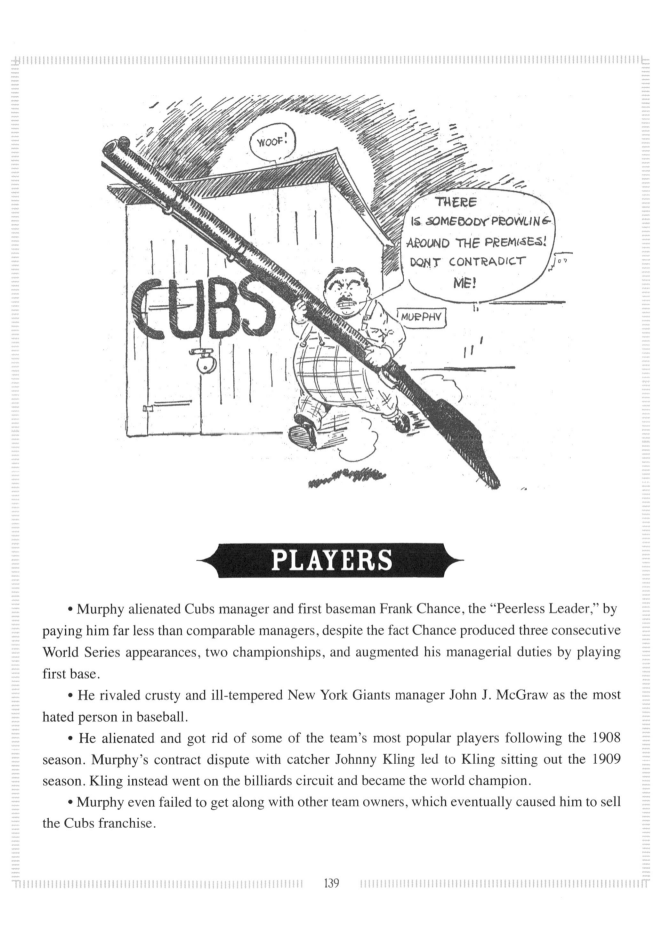

PLAYERS

• Murphy alienated Cubs manager and first baseman Frank Chance, the "Peerless Leader," by paying him far less than comparable managers, despite the fact Chance produced three consecutive World Series appearances, two championships, and augmented his managerial duties by playing first base.

• He rivaled crusty and ill-tempered New York Giants manager John J. McGraw as the most hated person in baseball.

• He alienated and got rid of some of the team's most popular players following the 1908 season. Murphy's contract dispute with catcher Johnny Kling led to Kling sitting out the 1909 season. Kling instead went on the billiards circuit and became the world champion.

• Murphy even failed to get along with other team owners, which eventually caused him to sell the Cubs franchise.

Murphy alienated fans in just about every way imaginable:

• He raised World Series ticket prices to unprecedented levels.

• He had barriers built at West Side Grounds to block the view of fans on nearby rooftops.

• He agitated for his players to disassociate from the West Side Rooters Social Club.

• He assigned the local media to the last row of the grandstands during the 1908 World Series.

The day after Murphy was excluded from Cohan's celebratory dinner, he blasted back with a caustic letter to fans, players, and anyone else who had dared question his actions. Murphy's letter was printed in every Chicago newspaper. This was the *Tribune*'s headline on Saturday, October 17, 1908:

"MURPHY ANSWERS CRITICS: BRANDS CHARGES AS ABSURD."
"President of Cubs Says Talk of World's Series Mismanagement
Is Unfair and Unwarranted by Facts."

DePorter poured over the letter, looking for clues. "The letter was a particularly mean-spirited response to complaints about his handling of the World Series," he said. "Here was a guy whose team had just won a second straight world championship, and he follows that up by blasting everyone, including the fans, in a very public way. Still, it wasn't until I reached the end of the letter that I realized Murphy was a hoodoo."

For DePorter, it was the closest he came to a "Eureka!" moment. Murphy's final words in the infamous letter said it all:

"ROME WAS NOT BUILT IN A DAY, AND IT TAKES TIME EVEN IN CHICAGO TO GET READY FOR A WORLD'S SERIES."

CHARLES W. MURPHY,
President, Chicago National League Baseball Club
October 17, 1908

DePorter was dumbfounded. The critics that Murphy attacked were not only Cubs fans, arguably the most renown in baseball, but also his own players and manager.

After months of research, DePorter knew it was time to look beyond 1908. Without question, disappointment had been the Cubs' common denominator in the years that followed, but failure came in many forms. DePorter first looked at the most offensive examples. He studied the events surrounding William Sianis and his goat in 1945. Then he looked at the haunting collapses in 1969, 1984, and 2003.

MURPHY HAD BEEN THERE ALL ALONG IN PLAIN SIGHT.

"Everywhere I looked, a Murphy was involved," DePorter said. "Like everyone else, I was familiar with Murphy's Law: Everything that can go wrong will go wrong, which obviously had described the Cubs since 1908. Murphy's letter was a 'knock-on-wood moment,' a clear hoodoo, given the timing and tone. But it was the infamous Sianis goat that confirmed that Murphy was the source of the greatest hoodoo of all time. It was Murphy all along."

Why look at the goat first? DePorter could start nowhere else. At least two generations of Cubs fans had come to believe the Sianis goat was the source of the team's cursed existence. First, as noted previously, any hoodoo having to do with a goat dated back to 1908. Second, DePorter found out all he needed to know when he learned the name of the original Sianis goat:

MURPHY

Next up: 1969. The Mets broadcaster who called the game in September 1969 when a black cat ran onto the field at Shea Stadium and seemingly taunted the Cubs?

BOB MURPHY

And the San Diego stadium where a ground ball scooted past Cubs first baseman Leon Durham in 1984, affording the Padres a break that helped them get to the World Series instead of the Cubs? The name of the stadium:

JACK MURPHY

DePorter even recalled a conversation about Game 6 of the 2003 National League Championship Series against Florida that turned against the Cubs on the Infamous Cubs Foul Ball. A prominent local celebrity and long-time Cubs fan told DePorter, "Every time I come to a big game like this, the Cubs lose." His name:

MURPHY

"At last: The answer to a century of frustration for Cubs fans," DePorter said. "Murphy was a hoodoo of epic proportions. Given everything he did in 1908, it's hard to imagine what else he might have done to seal the franchise's fate."

As it turned out, Murphy's letter to the newspapers was simply his public *coup de grace*.

"In 2003 I actually didn't think the link to Murphy was strong enough," DePorter said. "So I kept digging. I had established the Murphy connection to the Cubs' failures in 1984 and 1969. After the Infamous Cubs Foul Ball incident, I started wondering whether Murphy had any relationship to the 2003 Cubs season. A high-profile Chicagoan named Murphy admitted to me that he was not only at the 2003 game, but that he had been present for virtually every significant Cubs loss dating back to 1969. A number of other Murphys told me of being at the 2003 game, too.

"But what I found most interesting is that 2003 also happened to be the last year for Bob Murphy and Jack Murphy Stadium. And then, the saddest note of all, was the passing of Jim Murphy, the legendary owner of Murphy's Bleachers bar, who joined Harry in heaven that same year."

If that's not enough, DePorter came across these gems as well:

- In October 2003, Harvard University celebrated the fiftieth anniversary of the origin of the traditionally recognized version of Murphy's Law.
- And "Murphy's Law" a song by Murphy Lee, peaked at number 8 on the Billboard charts in October 2003.

JUST WHO WAS THE MAN WHO BECAME A HUNDRED-YEAR THORN IN THE CUBS PAWS?

Charles W. Murphy took an unconventional route to ownership of the Cubs. Born in Ohio in 1868, Murphy graduated from pharmacy school in Cincinnati, then went to work in a drugstore. Soon after, he changed careers, signing on with the Cincinnati Enquirer as a sportswriter. The newspaper was owned by Charles Phelps Taft, a half-brother to William Howard Taft, the twenty-seventh president of the United States and the tenth Chief Justice of the Supreme Court.

Murphy and Charles Taft became friends. In might be hard to put a price on friendship, but not in this case. Murphy wasn't particularly well-paid, and he certainly wasn't rich when he learned that the Cubs would be put up for sale. Murphy took a train to Chicago and, with Taft's financial backing, made an offer to Cubs owner James A. Hart.

On July 31, 1905, thanks to Taft's

$105,000 LOAN,

Murphy closed a deal to purchase the Cubs.

FROM THE FANOCRATIC CONVENTION.

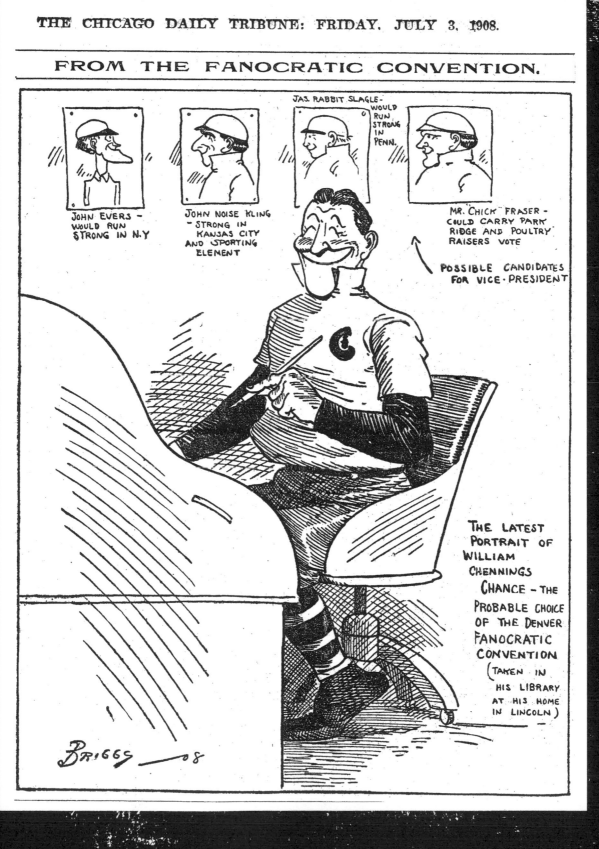

"All the personal popularity in the world gets the club owner nothing if his club is a loser," New York Giants owner John T. Brush, Murphy's onetime employer, told Murphy.

Gaining popularity was not important to Murphy. He was much more interested in winning and making money—not necessarily in that order. The Cubs were so successful so quickly under Murphy's ownership that he was able to pay back Taft within a year.

In 1905, the Cubs surpassed a half-million in attendance for the first time. And that was with a team that started the season 21-24 before catching fire and finishing in third place with a 92-61 record. The team rose from there until Murphy's unforgivable behavior created a hoodoo that transformed baseball's most accomplished franchise into sport's most fabled loser.

IT WAS CLEAR TO DEPORTER THAT BY DECODING MURPHY'S LAW HE HAD IDENTIFIED CRITICAL STRANDS OF THE DNA THAT FORMED THE CUBS' HOODOO.

"I knew Murphy's Law was the critical missing link between the franchise's greatest success and all the losing that followed," DePorter said. "What I didn't know at the time was whether there was more to the story."

DePorter was clear on one thing: The hoodoo had to be undone.

CHICAGO RECORD-HERALD.

OCTOBER 14, 1908

THE END OF THE BASEBALL EXCITEMENT—IF THE CUBS WIN TO-DAY.

CHAPTER 6

THE MURPHY'S LAW
DINNER

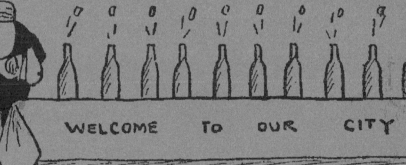

WELCOME   TO   OUR   CITY

CHICAGO DAILY NEWS

FRIDAY, FEBRUARY 14, 1908.

BASEBALL FANS HAVE HAD AN UNEASY REST.

THERE ARE LIMITS EVEN IN THE
FORTUNE TELLING BUSINESS

By 2007, DePorter had spent countless hours and dollars trying to reverse the curse on behalf of Cubs fans.

Indeed, that's how he saw his efforts. He was the conduit through which Cubs fans from around the world channeled their energy to rid the franchise of its tortured past.

When the destruction of the Infamous Cubs Foul Ball failed to produce the desired result in 2004, DePorter followed the advice of fans and turned what was left of the ball into an edible concoction to be devoured in 2005. However, those efforts served only to reverse droughts in Boston and on the South Side of Chicago.

DePorter's discovery of "Murphy's Law" confirmed what he had suspected all along: The Murphy hoodoo was connected to virtually everything that had happened to the Cubs since 1908.

DePorter knew some fans thought there was a natural progression to the curse-removing business. The Red Sox had the third-longest World Series drought, and they won in 2004. The White Sox had the second-longest drought, and they won in 2005. The Cubs had to be up next.

"I HAD HEARD ABOUT A THEORY THAT EVERYTHING HAD TO HAPPEN IN ORDER, AND THAT THE CUBS WERE THIRD IN LINE," DEPORTER SAID. "BUT I NEEDED OUTSIDE CONFIRMATION."

Who better to provide insight into the future than Nostradamus?

It wasn't until he happened upon one of Nostradamus's quatrains that DePorter understood that World Series championships in Boston and Chicago were predicted long ago as part of a established progression that would end with the Cubs winning a title, too.

Born in the early sixteenth century, Nostradamus made prophesies that were said to be "as poetic as they were cryptic." They were also known to conceal revelations of the future, many of which are harrowing. He wrote 942 quatrains that were organized into centuries, or groups of one hundred quatrains, save for one that had only forty-two.

The "Regimento do Astrolabio et do Quadrante," published in 1509, is considered to contain the earliest known work of Nostradamus. Given that his quatrains are thought to have predicted, among other things, the emergence of tyrants and natural disasters, his predictions regarding the Red Sox, White Sox, and Cubs are clearly within the bounds of his work.

What is obvious from looking at the following quatrain from Century IX, even to the untrained eye, is the pattern that has in fact emerged, thus confirming Nostradamus's remarkable prediction conceived five centuries earlier.

As DePorter notes, it references the Cubs, a goat, Harry Caray, and even the 2008 Major League Baseball All-Star team.

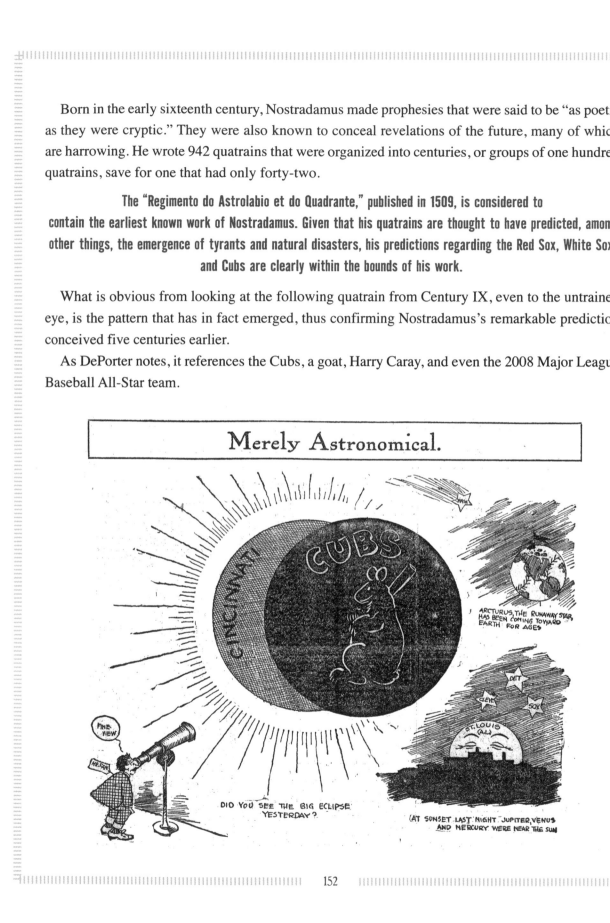

152

THE LESSER BEAR

Alruc(c)aba, Banat Nash al Bughra, Dhub (E/A)lesguar, Dubb al Aggbar, Kutb al Shamaliyy, Al Rakabah, VIII.26.1 De Caron es trouues en Barsellone

CARED ONES ENSURE TOWERS CAUSE NO BEARS TO SELL

VERSE IV.43

The Little Bears Cynosurae (Polestar) letter is to be subtracted.
Nostredame says he used the same method.
There will appear towards the
seven stars of Ursa Minor and Polaris
Not far from Cancer,
The Bearded Star
Susa, Siena, Boeotia, Great Rome
will die, the night having vanished
C6 Q

QUATRAIN 6.6

It will appear towards Ursa Minor,
Not far from Cancer, the bearded star:
Susa [NW Italy], Siena [central Italy], Boetia [SE Greece], Eretria [E. Greece],
The great one of Rome will die, the night dispersed.

At night they will think they have seen the sun,
when they see the half pig man:
Noise, screams, battles seen fought in the skies.
The animals will be heard to speak.
Nostradamus, 1555

QUATRAINS—CENTURY IX

3
The "great cow" at Racenna in great trouble,
Led by fifteen shut up at Fornase:
At Rome there will be born two double-headed monsters,
Blood, fire, flood, the greatest ones in space.

The English translated verse, taken from Century 2, Quatrain 62: "We must observe that the third antichrist as described by Nostradamus involves a relation of Alus of blood, or red, Mabus as white, and Perse of blue."

THE CHICAGO DAILY NEWS.

WEDNESDAY, OCTOBER 14, 1908.

CHICAGO CUBS WIN WORLD'S BASEBALL CHAMPIONSHIP

RIGHTFUL OCCUPANT OF FLATS WILL SOON PROVE TITLE.

Additionally, an English-translated verse taken from Century 2, Quatrain 62 (page 153) speaks directly to the progression of Red Sox, White Sox, and Cubs.

"The quatrains are pretty straightforward," DePorter said. "Nostradamus refers to 'Little Bears' at least four times, an obvious reference to the Cubs. The 'seven stars' refer to the 2008 All-Star Game that included a record seven Cubs. The bearded star is most certainly a goat. And the 'great cow' couldn't be any clearer—he's talking about Harry.

"And the last line of the translation lays it all out. Alus, or blood, comes first and corresponds to the Red Sox. Mabus, or white, comes next, and its symbolism is just as obvious regarding the White Sox. Perse, or blue, confirms the Cubs are the next to win. If you think about it, the progression makes perfect sense. Boston had the most recent title in 1918. The White Sox were next at 1917, and Cubs come next at 1908."

DePorter felt all along that Boston and the White Sox needed to eliminate their hoodoos first, which is why he helped those efforts. That way, a Cubs' World Series victory, as is only right and clearly foretold by Nostradamus, becomes the greatest show on Earth.

With all signs, old and new, pointing to an impending Cubs title, DePorter focused on repealing Murphy's Law.

In February 2007, he announced what became known as the "Murphy's Law Dinner," designed to reverse what Murphy himself had put in motion in 1908.

"After ninety-nine years we believed it was time to forgive Mr. Murphy and to invite his spirit back to the table," DePorter said.

2007 TOAST AND DINNER ITINERARY

*** FEBRUARY 14, 2007 ***

4:45 p.m. Two tables of twenty are set up in the dining room at Harry Caray's Italian Steakhouse in downtown Chicago, with one representative from each of the surnames and their guest at each table.

Each seat is set with a nametag, place card, and coin from 1907 or 1908.

5:00 p.m. Dinner participants and guests arrive.

Guests are served first course (Turtle Soup).

5:20 p.m. Cohan and Murphy leave dining room and go behind bar.

Dutchie Caray, Grant DePorter, Ryne Sandberg, John McDonough, and Bill Kurtis take the stage with Roe Conn to lead a toast.

5:25 p.m. Cohan gives toast welcoming guests to reenactment dinner, and welcomes Murphy, who was not invited to original dinner.

5:26 p.m. Murphy gives toast, forgiving Cohan for not inviting Murphy to the original dinner and lifting the curse of Murphy's Law from the Chicago Cubs.

5:30 p.m. Roe introduces Dutchie, who will lead another toast.

Dutchie gives speech, references historic dinner, and introduces DePorter, Sandberg, McDonough, and Kurtis to help her lead toast to Harry Caray.

Dutchie says, "Here's to Harry," and guests all raise their Budweiser to Harry.

5:32 p.m. Dutchie leads, "Take Me Out to the Ball Game," along with video of Harry singing on television monitors.

5:35 p.m. Cohan and Murphy descendants head back to the dining room.

Servers pop the champagne and serve all the guests a glass, for another toast.

5:40 p.m. The curse is lifted!

Coinciding with the ninth Annual Worldwide Toast to Harry Caray, descendants of players from the 1908 Cubs came from all over the country to attend the dinner. Murphy had so alienated the players that it made sense to include their representatives in the ceremonial exorcism. The only difference: This time Murphy was present.

The great-great nephew of Charles W. Murphy represented the former Cubs owner and read a proclamation on behalf of the Murphy family.

"On behalf of Charles, my great-great uncle, I hereby forgive Mr. Cohan and the rest of the guests, and I officially lift the curse of Murphy's Law," Mark Krudnick, of Downers Grove, Illinois, told the gathering.

GUESTS SHOUTED "GO CUBS!" AND THEN CONDUCTED A CHAMPAGNE TOAST.

DePorter left nothing to chance. Anyone driving a Model T, which was invented in 1908, received free valet parking. And guests sang, "Take Me Out to the Ball Game," which was written the same year.

RECTOR'S

CHICAGO

WORLD CHAMPION CHICAGO CUBS CELEBRATION DINNER
October 15, 1908

Hosted by Mr. George M. Cohan
Invited Guests: Mr. Chance, Mr. Tinker, Mr. Steinfeldt, Mr. Howard, Mr. Scheckard, Mr. Evers,
Mr. Moran, Mr. Williams, and special guest Mr. Charles W. Murphy

MENU

First Course
Turtle Soup $.40

Second Course
select one
Pâté de Foie Gras $1.00
(Since fois gras is currently illegal in Chicago, faux gras will be served)
Lettuce Salad $.40

Third Course
select one
Broiled Live Lobster $.80
Tenderloin Steak $.90
Half Chicken, Broiled $.75
Salmon, Broiled $.80

select one
Baked Potato $.20
American Asparagus $.60
Spinach $.40

Fourth Course

Coffee, per cup $.10

select one
Charlotte Russe $.25
Vanilla Ice Cream $.25

The event was a reenactment of Cohan's 1908 dinner, down to the menu items and prices.

"I'm here for those who believe," fifty-nine-year-old William Steinfeldt, the second cousin of third baseman Harry Steinfeldt, told *Chicago Sun-Times* writer Carol Slezak. **"But listen to this: Harry wore number 13 in the 1908 World Series, and my father was born on the thirteenth, and I was born on the thirteenth, and my own son was born on the thirteenth. So there's some numerology there that might mean something too."**

The numerology that mattered in 2007 involved the number nine—as in ninety-nine years since the Cubs last won a World Series.

Was there anything worse than an owner alienating his players only hours after a World Series victory? Despite his best efforts, DePorter had the nagging sense that there was indeed one thing even more egregious.

CHAPTER 7

THE ROOTERS
REORGANIZE

CUBS HOODOO DNA FULLY SEQUENCED

GUESS WHO'S HERE?

The 2007 Major League Baseball season still had weeks remaining when ninety-nine turned into one hundred for Cubs fans. To fully appreciate the distance between 1908 and 2008 you have to realize what's taken place since the Cubs last won a World Series. A sampling:

Prohibition was instituted—and repealed.

Harry Caray was born and died—without seeing a Cubs' World Series championship.

Haley's Comet passed Earth—twice.

Wrigley Field was built, and grew up to be the oldest ballpark in the National League.

George Burns celebrated his tenth, twentieth, thirtieth, fortieth, fiftieth, sixtieth, seventieth, eightieth, ninetieth, and one-hundredth birthdays.

The NBA, NHL and NFL were formed; Chicago teams won championships in all three.

The Titanic was built, set sail, sank, was discovered at the bottom of the Atlantic Ocean, and became the subject of major motion pictures, the latter giving Cubs fans hope that something that finishes on the bottom can come out on top.

Alaska, Arizona, Hawaii, Oklahoma, and New Mexico were added to the United States.

As the 2007 season got underway, DePorter, like every other Cubs fan, thought the curse finally had been reversed. But something in the back of Grant's mind kept him returning time and again to that stack of hundred-year old newspapers.

Clearly Murphy was at the center of the hoodoo.

DePorter had as many as thirty different themes operating in the early days of his research. Eventually, two dominant themes emerged. One of those was

MURPHY

who was the key to the Cubs' decline after 1908, and the other was the

WEST SIDE ROOTERS SOCIAL CLUB,

which was the key to the Cubs' success in 1908.

The fact Murphy had something less than warm feelings for the Rooters only strengthened the case for both themes.

In the end, however, it all came down to Murphy.

As a result, eliminating his hoodoo was a process, not a single act. Murphy was all over the 2003 foul-ball incident, which meant the ball had to be destroyed. Turning what remained of the ball into marinara sauce was another layer in undoing all that Murphy had put in place. So too was the decoding of Murphy's Law, and the dinner that removed the stratum related to Cubs players.

All of which led DePorter to the final act in the exorcism: Reorganizing the West Side Rooters Social Club.

When the Red Sox won the 2004 World Series, DePorter knew Cubs fans were at least partially responsible. He had invited Boston and Chicago White Sox fans to be on hand for the destruction of the Infamous Cubs Foul Ball, and later that year helped orchestrate a curse-ending ceremony at Fenway Park that featured pieces of the ball. Once more, however, DePorter's sixth sense told him there was something more to the story.

"When Boston ended its eighty-sixth-year drought, I wanted to know what their fans thought was the key to the team finally winning," DePorter said. "What I found is that Red Sox fans believed the team's success was directly related to bringing back the Royal Rooters and their theme song, 'Tessie.'"

The Royal Rooters had not been active since 1918, the same year the Red Sox had last won a World Series. Not only that, but a band called the "Dropkick Murphys" re-recorded "Tessie," which was a song from the Broadway musical, The Silver Slipper.

Inside Boston's front office, the connection between "Tessie," the Royal Rooters, and not one, but two World Series titles—the Red Sox won again in 2007—is considered something more than a mere coincidence.

"Don't tell me it is not connected," Dr. Charles Steinberg, senior vice president of public affairs for the Red Sox, said in the movie, *Rooters: Birth of the Red Sox Nation*.

"Now we brought back a song that was associated with the first five world championships. When that disappeared, so did the world championships. Then the song reappeared, and we won a world championship. You figure it out."

That's exactly what DePorter planned to do.

"I went back to see what parallel organization existed for the Chicago Cubs in 1908," DePorter said. "And sure enough, it was the West Side Rooters Social Club, which I had come across in my research. I found it more than a little interesting that the West Side Rooters, like Boston's Royal Rooters, were disbanded following the last World Series title of their respective teams."

The West Side Rooters Social Club was founded on January 17, 1908, to the delight of fans and Cubs players. At the time, the Royal Rooters had been around since 1903, and the White Sox had their own organized group as well. Cubs shortstop Joe Tinker became chairman of the West Side Rooters, and manager Frank Chance and other players were deeply involved as well.

A headline in the *Chicago Tribune* on January 18, 1908, said it all:

"NEW CLUB FORMED TO HOLD WINTER ENTERTAINMENTS AND MAKE NOISE DURING BASEBALL SEASON"

One of the first things the Rooters did was to invite Murphy to be a part of the club. Murphy declined the offer, although he did send fifty dollars to help the new organization.

The West Side Rooters' war cry was of unknown origin: "OOF WAH!" Not exactly as refined as "Tessie," but effective nonetheless. The club practiced what it called "scientific rooting," which was essentially directing cheers toward the Cubs in an organized – thus more powerful – way.

Not even a severe February snowstorm could dampen the Rooters' enthusiasm. The *Tribune* account told of "wretched weather," but the Rooters' February 18 event was well-attended. It featured speeches by Rooters president Thomas Johnson, as well as talks by Murphy and White Sox owner Charles Comiskey. Comiskey told fans that if his team couldn't win, then "my next best wish is for the Cubs to land first honors and keep them in Chicago."

When the Rooters hosted a reception and ball at Princess Hall on West Madison Street four months after the club's creation, more than 1,000 people showed up.

Within weeks of Murphy's appearance at the mid-February Rooters stag, the Cubs president revealed his true feelings, which had never been far from the surface to begin with, and set in motion a hoodoo of unrelenting proportions.

Murphy clashed with Tinker, one of his star players, on the issue of merchants providing champagne and edibles for a Rooters function. In short order, the relationship between management and fans was defined. From DePorter's perspective, that fact alone provided the basis of a punishing hoodoo.

It's one thing to offend your players, which Murphy did—and DePorter tried to undo with the 2007 Murphy's Dinner. But it's clearly of a different magnitude to become party to conflict, real or imagined, with your fan base, particularly in the aftermath of a World Series title and prior to another championship season.

Murphy's lack of respect for the Rooters was exacerbated by the almost spiritual connection that existed in 1908—and throughout history for that matter—between Cubs players and the team's fans. The metaphysical force, or hoodoo, that Murphy put in motion obviously became strongest when emotions were the most intense.

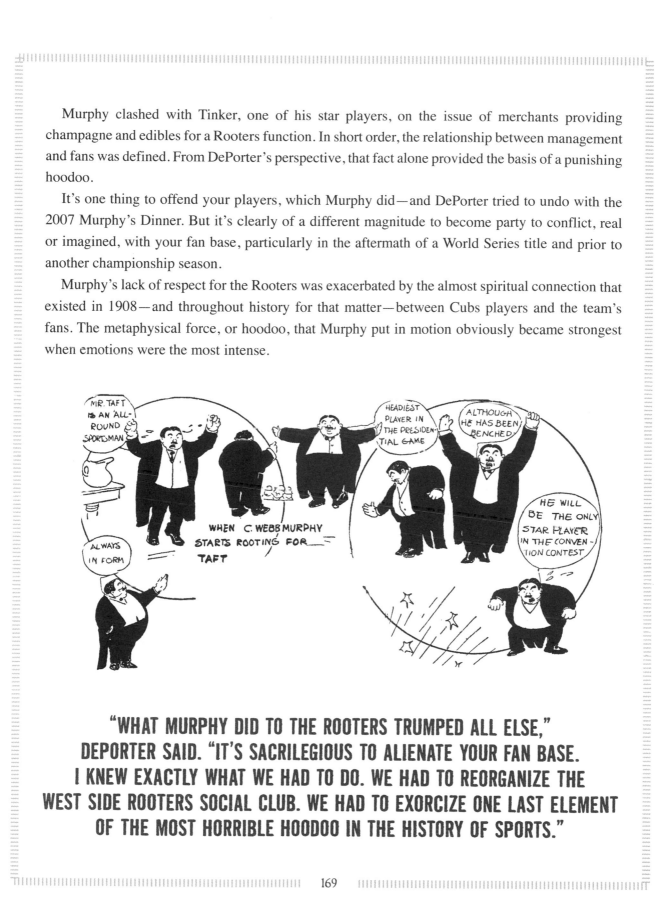

**"WHAT MURPHY DID TO THE ROOTERS TRUMPED ALL ELSE,"
DEPORTER SAID. "IT'S SACRILEGIOUS TO ALIENATE YOUR FAN BASE.
I KNEW EXACTLY WHAT WE HAD TO DO. WE HAD TO REORGANIZE THE
WEST SIDE ROOTERS SOCIAL CLUB. WE HAD TO EXORCIZE ONE LAST ELEMENT
OF THE MOST HORRIBLE HOODOO IN THE HISTORY OF SPORTS."**

SUGGESTIONS FOR BUTTON DESIGNS FOR THE WEST SIDE ROOTERS' ASSOCIATION.

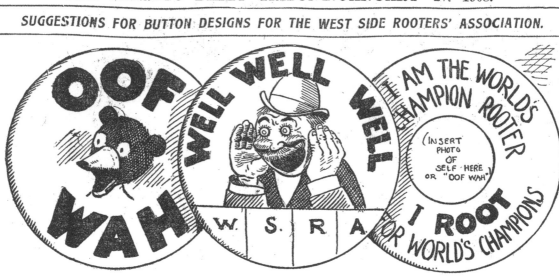

As he had done since the original Toast to Harry in 1999, DePorter organized with an attention to detail that could only come from a man who had spent countless hours and dollars in the singular pursuit of closure for Cubs fans the world over.

He assembled a star-studded lineup, with "Mr. Cub," Ernie Banks, the obvious choice as Rooters chairman. With Banks in place, DePorter called on another Cubs Hall of Famer, Ryne Sandberg, to assume the position of secretary. Fans seeking membership through the club's Internet site—westsiderooters.com—receive a personal letter from Sandberg welcoming them into the club.

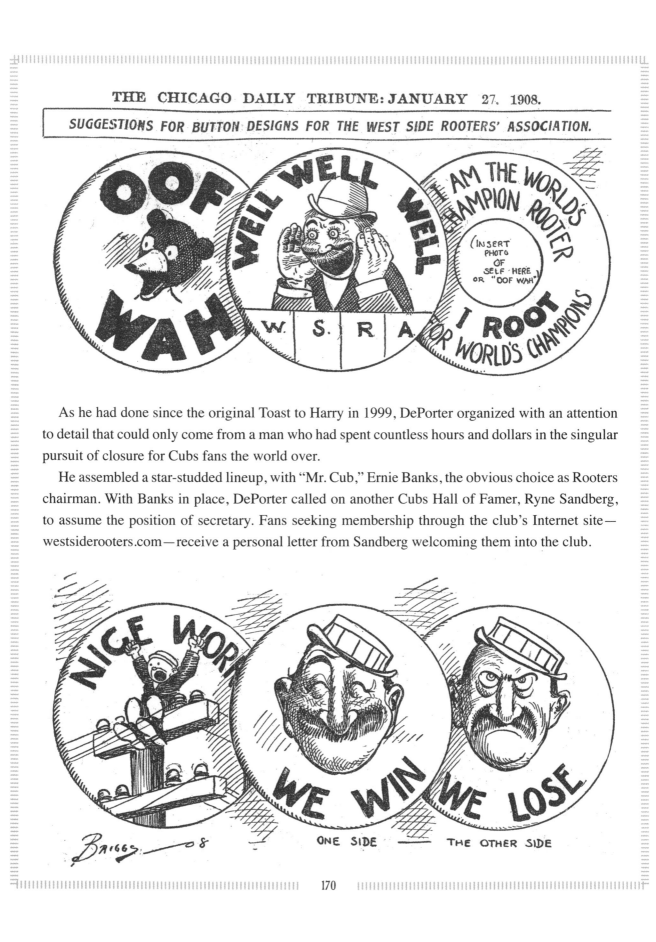

Staying true to form, that was just the beginning for DePorter. After more than four years working to undo Murphy's hoodoo, he left nothing to chance. The club's first official meeting was held June 18, 2008, at Harry Caray's Tavern, with Banks presiding.

Buttons were made and distributed as fans from every corner of the Cubs kingdom came on board. Within two weeks, thousands had joined the club, including Cubs Hall of Fame players, members of the media, and Cubs management. The West Side Rooters Social Club continued to surge in membership as the team surged to the top of the National League Central division.

DePorter then organized a reenactment of one of the Rooters' Tallyho parades of 1908, duplicating the event right down to the date: 08.08.08.

A little more than a month later, the 2008 West Side Rooters recreated the dance thrown by their 1908 brethren.

At long last it seemed that DePorter and the Cubs fans he represented on a journey that spanned one hundred years could rest easy in the knowledge that all that had to be done had been done.

From the data dig through countless newspapers, magazines, and books, to the masterfully executed public events designed to eliminate the hoodoo, the crowning blow in a crowning achievement had been landed with the reorganization of the West Side Rooters.

Clearly, and with the fog of history removed, only one eight remained between the Cubs and the World Series. And that was 2008.

Unless of course, it turned out to be next year.

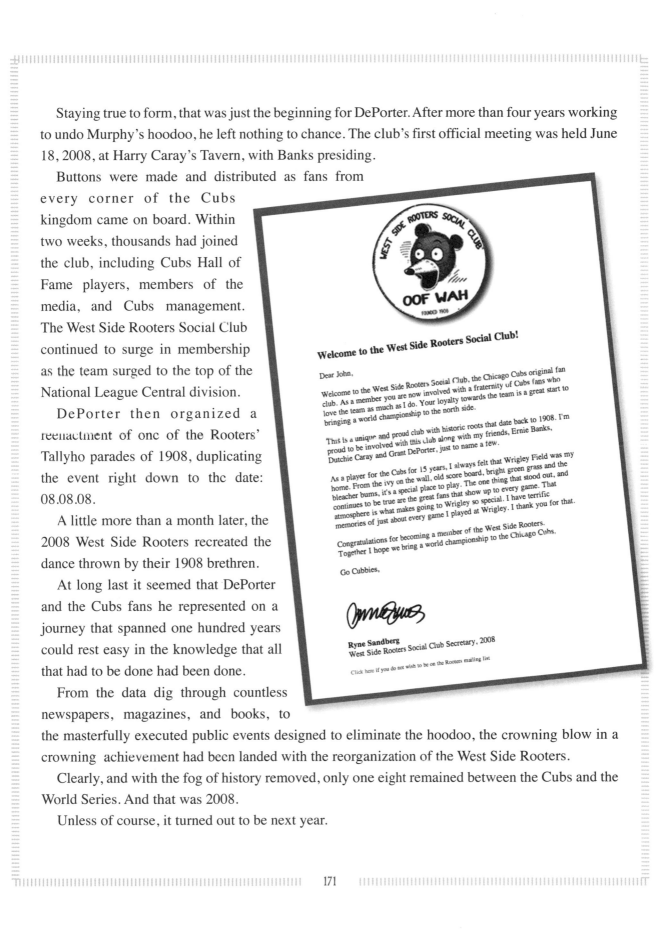

Welcome to the West Side Rooters Social Club!

Dear John,

Welcome to the West Side Rooters Social Club, the Chicago Cubs original fan club. As a member you are now involved with a fraternity of Cubs fans who love the team as much as I do. Your loyalty towards the team is a great start to bringing a world championship to the north side.

This is a unique and proud club with historic roots that date back to 1908. I'm proud to be involved with this club along with my friends, Ernie Banks, Dutchie Caray and Grant DePorter, just to name a few.

As a player for the Cubs for 15 years, I always felt that Wrigley Field was my home. From the ivy on the wall, old score board, bright green grass and the bleacher bums, it's a special place to play. The one thing that stood out, and continues to be true are the great fans that show up to every game. That atmosphere is what makes going to Wrigley so special. I have terrific memories of just about every game I played at Wrigley. I thank you for that.

Congratulations for becoming a member of the West Side Rooters. Together I hope we bring a world championship to the Chicago Cubs.

Go Cubbies,

Ryne Sandberg
West Side Rooters Social Club Secretary, 2008

Click here if you do not wish to be on the Rooters mailing list

WEST SIDE ROOTERS
SOCIAL CLUB

1908 COMMITTEE

CHAIRMAN
JOE TINKER
Hall of Fame Cub

PRESIDENT
THOMAS JOHNSON

TREASURER
AL PHILLIPS

SECRETARY
AL GERMANN

TODAY'S COMMITTEE
REVIVED IN 2008

CHAIRMAN
ERNIE BANKS
Hall of Fame Cub

PRESIDENT
GRANT DEPORTER

TREASURER
DUTCHIE CARAY

SECRETARY
RYNE SANDBERG
Hall of Fame Cub

ASSISTANT SECRETARY
ROB GLAUBKE
Cubs Fan and Website Designer

SERGEANT AT ARMS
RONNIE WOO WOO

ROOTERS STAFF
WILL BYINGTON
Official Rooters Photographer

Cub Rooters!
GO TO
DETROIT
VIA THE
WABASH
$8.25 ROUND TRIP
Good Going October 9.
Good Returning Until October 11, Inclusive.
CHOICE OF THREE TRAINS.
WABASH OFFICE, 109 Adams Street,
Or tickets can be purchased and trains taken at 47th St.
and 63d St. (Englewood.)

THE POWER OF 8

1908
CUBS WIN THEIR LAST WORLD SERIES

08.08.1908
WEST SIDE ROOTERS TALLYHO PARADE

08.08.1988
FIRST NIGHT GAME AT WRIGLEY FIELD

1998
HARRY GOES TO HEAVEN

MURPHY'S LAW SONG REACHED **NO. 8**
ON BILLBOARD CHARTS IN 2003

BOSTON BECOMES FIRST TEAM TO WIN LAST **8** GAMES;
WINS 2004 WORLD SERIES

CHICAGO WHITE SOX BECOME SECOND TEAM TO WIN LAST **8** GAMES;
WINS 2005 WORLD SERIES

08.08.2008
WEST SIDE ROOTERS TALLYHO PARADE

GOING BY TALLYHO

The Winning Ticket.

AUTHOR BIOGRAPHIES

GRANT DEPORTER is president of Harry Caray's Restaurant Group. A graduate of Cornell University with an MBA from Duke University, he has led the company's expansion to include seven establishments around Chicagoland. Grant became known to baseball fans around the world when he purchased and then destroyed the Infamous Cubs Foul Ball. He is president of the West Side Rooters Social Club, the original Cubs fan club that he revived in 2008. He has served on committees and boards of several Chicago area civic organizations, and has chaired the Illinois Restaurant Association, Illinois Tourism Alliance, Chicago Gateway Green, and the Magnificent Mile Lights Festival. He remembers going to his first Cubs game at Wrigley Field in 1969 when he was four years old. He remembers how loud the crowd was. How tall, too—much of his view was obscured by cheering fans jumping out of their seats. He since has gained a better perspective—with a Cubs World Series championship clearly in his sights. He and his wife Joanna have two children.

ELLIOTT HARRIS has been the Quick Hits columnist in the *Chicago Sun-Times* sports section since the feature's inception in September 1998. That was when Sammy Sosa was on his way to hitting sixty-six home runs, and the Cubs were on their way to the postseason (though not to winning the World Series, or even reaching it). Before joining the *Sun-Times* in 1979, he worked at the *Miami (FL) News*, *Columbia (MO) Daily Tribune*, and *Fort Worth (TX) Star-Telegram*. A graduate of the University of Missouri, he is a native of St. Louis (which some Cubs fans may regard as a hoodoo in itself). He and his wife Sue have two children.

MARK VANCIL is president and principal of Rare Air Media, a Winnetka, Illinois-based publishing and communications company. Rare Air Books, a division of Rare Air Media, has produced dozens of award-winning titles—including five *New York Times'* bestsellers—with a variety of high-profile individuals, professional organizations, and corporations, among them Michael Jordan, Brett Favre, Dan Marino, John Elway, Major League Baseball, National Basketball Association, National Football League, New York Yankees, Johnny Cash, Nike/Brand Jordan, MasterCard International, Hard Rock Café, McDonald's, and Pepsi Co.

In addition to a number of titles in development, Rare Air is currently producing *Yankee Stadium: The Official Retrospective* (spring 2009). Mr. Vancil wrote *Leadership: Leading From Within with Alford McMichael* (Simon & Schuster, May 2008), with the 14th Sergeant Major and first African-American of the United States Marine Corp.; and David Falk's *The Bald Truth* (Simon & Schuster, February 2009), a business book about Falk's principles and how he applied them at the top of the sports and entertainment world.

Mr. Vancil is founding partner and principal of MareMark Entertainment in Los Angeles, California. In addition to providing product placement expertise to clients such as Toyota and BMW, the agency develops branded content for film and television.

The Mark and Laura Vancil Family Foundation is dedicated to assisting children and family-related causes, including the Women and Children's Shelter, Hospice, and the National Breast Cancer Coalition.

Mark and Laura Vancil have four children—Alexandra, Samantha, Isabella, and Jonah.